HEDONISM hēd'n iz'əm / *n.*
1: the doctrine that pleasure or happiness is
the sole or chief good in life. 2: a lifestyle
of enlightenment and enjoyment.
3: a most pleasurable outlook.

THE HEDONISM
HANDBOOK

The HEDONISM *Handbook*

MASTERING THE LOST ARTS OF LEISURE AND PLEASURE

Michael Flocker

DA CAPO PRESS
A Member of the Perseus Books Group

First printing, August 2004
ISBN 0-306-81414-5

Da Capo Press is a member of the Perseus Books Group

Visit us on the World Wide Web at www.dacapopress.com

Da Capo Press books are available at special discounts for bulk purchases in the U.S. by corporations, institutions, and other organizations. For more information, please contact the Special Markets Department, Perseus Books Group, 11 Cambridge Center, Cambridge, MA 02142, or call (800)-255-1514 or e-mail special.markets@perseusbooks.com.

Cover design by George Restrepo
Text design by George Restrepo
Set in Bodoni Old Face BE Regular

1 2 3 4 5 6 7 8 9 10 – 07 06 05 04

Contents

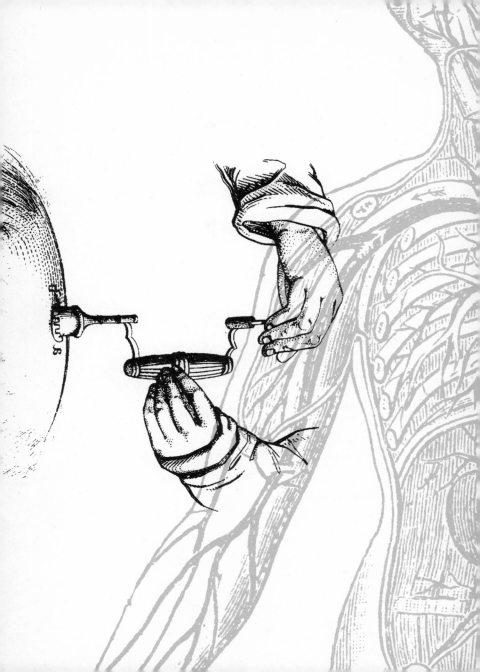

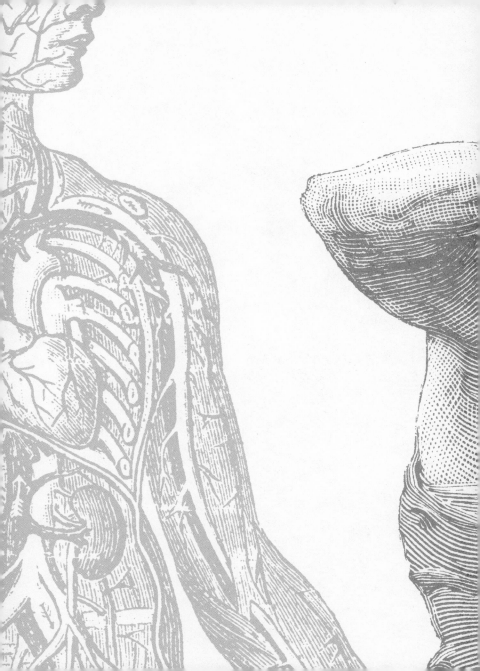

Introduction

"NO HUMAN THING IS OF SERIOUS IMPORTANCE."
— *Plato*

YES, YES, I KNOW, CIGARETTES ARE BAD AND SEX CAN BE dangerous. But a strange and disturbing epidemic seems to have gripped the nation of late in the form of a most ludicrous assumption: "If you avoid all things pleasurable, you will live a long and happy life." But can happiness really be found scampering along on a treadmill in a smoke-free environment, Palm Pilot in hand, chasing after the capitalist ideal? Are sixty-hour work weeks, bulging stock portfolios and a packed agenda really the keys to the good life? I think not.

In recent years, the Western world has become a kaleidoscopic pastiche of bright lights, media manipulation, global gossip and desperate competition. People stare at computer screens all day, eat lunch at their desks, plan their daily schedules on hand-held devices, and make "play dates" for their children. Obsessed with becoming richer, thinner, more successful and, implausibly, even younger, millions of us deprive ourselves on a daily basis of the one thing we misguidedly believe we are rushing toward—the good life. After a long workday, we rush home to watch what is amusingly known as "reality television" only to return to the office the next day to discuss the startling twists and turns in the manufactured realities of strangers, our own lives reduced to a mere afterthought. This hectic pace is sometimes cleverly offset by regularly scheduled workouts, carb-free diets, a stiff shot of wheatgrass juice and two weeks of "vacation" carefully planned online. Happiness, you see?

Added to this lovely cocktail of confusion are increasingly capricious laws that have smokers huddling on sidewalks, fast-food restaurants disclosing the shocking news that their food may make you fat, e-mails being monitored, park benches sporting dividers to prevent reclining, and various restrictions on language and lifestyle in general. It would seem that we—the masses—have become little more than fat baby ducks who need to be shepherded through life lest we veer off into a dangerous realm of personal responsibility and free will.

At some point, "the good life" became some distantly imagined finish line that could only be reached through psychotic effort and willful determination. Like overcaffeinated hamsters on a wheel, we began running, sweating, sacrificing and panicking. The weight may be lost, but the self-loathing remains. The promotion may be earned, but the expenses keep rising. And despite all outward successes, the inner feelings of inadequacy and the disapproving sneers of the neighbors seem to become magnified. Could there possibly be something wrong with this master plan? Is there something out there, some lost key to the kingdom of happiness that is being overlooked? You bet your ass there is.

It's called pleasure. And whatever happened to pleasure? *The Oxford American Dictionary* defines *happy* as, "feeling or showing pleasure or contentment." To *enjoy* is "to get pleasure from." So, it would seem that happiness and enjoyment are rooted in the very principle of pleasure, which is currently on the brink of extinction. And pleasure has always been at the very heart of hedonism since the very notion first came into being back in the days of ancient Greece.

It is no coincidence that in times of great pressure, stress and strain, people tend to look for means of relief and escape. But if these moments of glorious indulgence are weighed down with unrealistic expectations or feelings of desperation, they often backfire because they tip the scales and throw off the cosmic balance of life. You can't run a marathon and then decide to suddenly get hammered. Bad things will surely happen. You can't fast for a month and then eat a whole cake. And you can't deprive yourself of pleasure and bliss for years, striving to become a superstar, only to try to escape from all the pressure by going on a messy crack bender. The trick is to pace yourself.

Eat the cake, drink the wine, lie in a hammock and stare at the stars with the hottie you picked up on the beach, but don't try to jam it all into a tightly-scheduled, six-day "vacation." If you give in to beauty, pleasure and self-indulgence on a daily basis, not only will you be happier day-to-day, you will be less likely to go off the deep end when it all gets too much and you finally cave in. One must practice the art of hedonism regularly to get really good at it.

By most definitions, *hedonism* is considered a lifestyle in which pleasure and happiness are the ultimate goals in life. A *hedonist* is one who seeks pleasure and avoids pain above all else. And somehow, this lovely and charming premise has been twisted and perverted to the point where it actually has negative connotations in the minds of many. But are the pursuit of pleasure and the avoidance of pain really such bad things? Don't babies, universally considered to be the purest of all beings, gravitate to the warmth and satisfaction of the bosom? Don't they wail at the discomfort of a full diaper and an itchy bunghole? Of course they do. They haven't been programmed to discipline themselves into a ridiculous, unnatural and miserable state of Spartan self-denial.

Pleasure is good. Eden was fun. Excess may be bad, but

self-deprivation is just stupid. To live a life consisting only of hard work, virtue, sacrifice and self-discipline is to be a martyr, and martyrs make lousy lovers, friends and party guests. Of course, any good thing taken to the extreme inevitably turns bad, but when the true principles of hedonism are employed on a daily basis, the result is a happy person. Granted, that happy person will undoubtedly piss off the martyr next door, but a truly happy person has no interest in such dreary characters.

The truth is, we live in an age of manufactured fear. Television reports warn of killer escalators, allergic lovers and undetectable underpants cameras. Man smokes joint and jumps out window! Woman develops laugh lines and loses job! Bride orders dessert and is ditched by groom! Well, yeah, it's a treacherous world out there, but sometimes you just have to take a chance. Cigarettes may be bad for you, but so is getting hit by a bus. Life is full of surprises and there are no guarantees, but one thing is certain: A life lived without pleasure, beauty and a sensible degree of self-indulgence is a sad and wasted one. Despite the ranting of religious extremists, life coaches and jaded psychologists, it's okay to have a good time.

Of course, not everyone appreciates happiness and freedom in others, and such concepts tend to ruffle the stiff feathers of our more conservative friends who race forward, fingers wagging, with dire warnings of slippery downward spirals and weepy tales of disintegrating families. It is true that throughout history, in various eras, people often dismissed the perils and dangers of excess, especially at times when life seemed fleeting and tenuous. "Live for today" became the battle cry for those who were suspicious of what tomorrow might bring. But if the endless parade of highly publicized tragedies has taught us anything over the years, it is that there is a limit to all things. So, yes, the consequences of excess must always be considered, but there's a lot of wiggle room between an Amish dinner and a pool party at Caligula's place.

In the current climate, the entire world finds itself in a most precarious era. Dangers abound, natural disasters loom and then strike, and at times the entire world structure seems no more stable than a house of cards. But it is far too simplistic to believe that in such times all the world's citizens simply reach for the hookah pipe. On the contrary, people react in very different ways to feelings of instability. Some cling more fervently to their faith, others lower their heads and plow ahead, believing they can control the world by controlling their careers, their bodies or their finances. And then there are those whose instincts lead them out onto life's patio for a long, slow dance. In the minds of these people, Peggy Lee can be heard in the distance lazily cooing, "Is That All There Is?" Those are the people you want to hang out with.

It's never too late to deprogram yourself, unplug, join the party and just say no.

A History of Hedonism

I

"PLEASURE IS THE BEGINNING AND THE END OF LIVING HAPPILY."

— Epicurus

IN THE BEGINNING...

IN ORDER TO GRASP THE TRUE MEANING OF HEDONISM, IT IS
necessary to travel back in time to ancient Greece where
the concept was first defined. Of course, the Greeks
didn't invent the good times, and mankind has always
had a healthy appetite for all things pleasurable. Long
before the Golden Age, the Mesopotamians, Chinese and
Egyptians were grinding up poppies, the Incas were
munching on coca leaves, everyone was sexing it up and
the lure of the midday nap in the sun was pretty much
universal. The fact that these ancient peoples all gravitated toward such earthly pleasures is not an indication that
they were lazy, debauched or by today's standards criminals on the loose. On the contrary, they were all tuned
in to the most human of inclinations, the
perfectly natural desire to attain a simple state of
peaceful bliss.

By the mid-400s B.C., Greece was at the height of its
Hellenistic age, and the Greek people considered themselves to be superior to the crass "barbarians" who lum-
bered about the rest of the globe. The Greeks had
elevated civilization not only by inventing democracy,
but also by striving to capture the ideal of beauty
through art, experience and architecture. Music, painting, poetry and sculpture became highly revered, and
drama itself was born as tragedies and comedies were
performed at religious festivals. And Greek architecture,

with its emphasis on the agora, or meeting place, provided a perfect setting for discourse and debate, which in turn gave rise to the great age of the philosophers.

It was Socrates, who had an unusual gift for brevity, who posed the question to his students, "What is good?" It is widely believed that it was Aristippus of Cyrene (c.435-360) who concluded that good was simply pleasure (*hêdonê*). This theory was later elaborated on by an Athenian named Epicurus (341-270), who taught from his tranquil garden that the point of all one's actions should be to attain pleasure, and that pleasure was the highest good. He believed that only by conquering one's fears of the gods and of death could one find the true path to happiness. But Epicurus was not reckless or shortsighted in his teachings. He warned that a wise person will eschew those pleasures that may ultimately lead to pain. Balance was the key, and the pursuit of pleasure brought with it an implied sense of responsibility.

By 146 B.C., the Romans had taken control of Greece, but Alexander the Great's conquest of Persia had ensured that Greek ideas and the Greek way of life had spread throughout Egypt and the near East. Though the Romans had a culture distinct unto themselves, they had no problems with the Epicurean school of thought. In fact, they raised the cult of pleasure to new heights. At its peak in the A.D. 100s, the Roman Empire contained roughly half of Europe, a large part of the Middle East

and the coastal regions of northern Africa. Rome was the capital, and with nearly a million inhabitants, it was the largest and most spectacular city in the world. And the Romans themselves were a randy band of raucous hedonists.

Emperors and members of the upper classes paid for the construction of theaters, sports arenas and public baths of marble and gold where members of all social classes could mingle and tingle in various ways. Though the baths provided the setting for all sorts of naughty pleasures, the real underlying purpose was to encourage bathing and improve public hygiene. When they weren't busy floating through the cleansing pools of water or sweating out the previous night's party at the steam baths, both men and women wore the customary, easy-access tunic, modestly covered by a toga. The loose and flowing gowns were not only liberating and sensuous, but they also encouraged the erotic tug of gravity and a sudden breeze to stir things up, which in turn kept the lively Romans on their toes. During the A.D. 100s, celebrations and "religious" festivals in honor of the gods had become so numerous that the emperor Marcus Aurelius finally had to step in and limit them to a sensible maximum of 135 per year.

Over time, the Roman upper classes had also turned dining into an art form, feasting on several courses of the most exotic foods and spices available. Eggs, fruits and shellfish were followed by a main course of meat, fish or fowl and honey-sweetened cakes. All of these delights were washed down with copious amounts of wine, as the science of fermentation had now been securely mastered, and, of course, no Dionysian orgy would be complete without lots of sex with slaves, siblings and senators' wives. Ah, the good old days.

Of course, the Roman Empire eventually collapsed, and those who favored a more disciplined existence were quick to claim that decadence was the cause. And though it may be true that a raging hangover might impair one's ability to govern efficiently, hedonism was not the cause of the grand unraveling. Among many other factors, the great empire had simply overextended itself, and its vast territories with their multitude of cultures, religions, languages and mass migrations had become too large to manage under a single system of common law and government. And though there are lessons to be drawn from the fall of an empire, the suppression of personal freedoms and pleasures will never prevent the chaos and destruction that can be wrought by misguided politics and extremist religions.

A BRIEF TOUR OF HISTORIC EXCESSES

Ancient Greece and Rome are not alone in the grand pantheon of historic eras when the masses decided it was time to cut loose, though they do retain a certain debauched cache in the collective unconscious. As the pendulum of history swings casually to and fro, politics, social upheaval and religious fervor tend to produce reactions in the lives of individuals, and thus great shifts occur in the realms of popular art, literature and lifestyle of the masses. Some examples:

PARIS IN THE 1800S

After the Revolution and Napoleon's boo-boo at Waterloo, Parisian bohemianism was on the rise. France had colonized Algeria and hashish was said to have replaced champagne among the intellectual set. Balzac, Flaubert and Dumas all wrote about their exposure to and experimentation with the newly fashionable drug, and the scientific community began researching its medicinal merits.

THE CALIFORNIA GOLD RUSH

Dreams of gold and the quest for instant riches in the mid-nineteenth century lured many from comfortable environments in the East to harsh camp conditions in California. Brothels, saloons and gambling offered some respite from the gloomy and barren existence, and the introduction of opium by Chinese immigrants drew many disillusioned miners to the satin pillow.

EDWARDIAN ENGLAND

Irony became fashionable in an uptight society as sexual intrigue got saucier behind closed doors, upper class ladies hid body piercings, the international opium trade expanded and the hypodermic needle was introduced. Hypocrisy and denial made hedonism more thrilling than ever.

WEIMAR GERMANY

The destruction and economic instability in the wake of World War I stimulated the pleasure impulse among the youth. The sun was worshipped along with the naked body, cabaret and modern art; Bauhaus and Dadaism horrified traditionalists; cinema was born and the upcoming backlash loomed ominously.

THE ROARING TWENTIES

Prohibition backfired big-time and America began to swing like never before. Flappers, speakeasies, bootleggers, jazz and gangsters dominated the headlines, and an international community of expatriate authors documented their decadent travels abroad.

THE SWINGING SIXTIES

"Turn On, Tune In and Drop Out" became the mantra as an entire generation rejected conformity. The psychedelic age ushered in free love, self-destructive rock stars and dreams of peace as flowers were stuffed inside rifles and pop culture was hijacked by the young. Eastern philosophies, hallucinogens, long hair and political protest were all embraced in the pursuit of nirvana.

STUDIO 54

A glittering crescent moon with a coke spoon was suspended over semi-clad celebrities shagging busboys as New York's Bacchanalian hot spot defined the '70s. Excess was in as the famous and the infamous rubbed elbows and other things amidst a barrage of disco beats and flashing lights. Again, ominous developments loomed on the horizon, but in this arena, only the present moment mattered.

"The road of excess leads to the palace of wisdom."
—*William Blake*

HISTORY'S MOST CELEBRATED HEDONISTS — ROYAL REVELERS

Lest the impression be given that the history of hedonism is solely based on intoxication, a brief review of some of history's more colorful trailblazers may be in order. Of course, the fun ones are those who went to extremes, and while some of the characters listed below may well have been complete loons, their peculiar proclivities and admirable insistence on having their desires fully sated make them worthy of consideration, if only for a good chuckle.

CLEOPATRA (69 B.C.–30 B.C.)

Far from being the great beauty of legend, the homely Cleopatra was only seventeen or eighteen when she inherited the throne of Egypt and began her legendary reign as one of history's greatest seductresses. Despite her big nose, she was quickly married—mind you, it was to her twelve-year-old brother, but why judge? Her reign was a tricky one, and after being driven from power she was soon restored to the throne by her lover Julius Caesar. When her husband-brother was killed, she promptly married her other twelve-year-old brother. Cleo soon had a baby who looked oddly Roman, and then she and the already-married Caesar spent a couple of sexy years living it up in Rome. But when he got stabbed to death, she hightailed it back to Egypt, where she had her latest husband-brother poisoned to death. In 42 B.C., when the newly empowered Mark Antony summoned her to modern-day Turkey for questioning, she arrived on a barge with purple sails and silver oars. She reclined beneath a golden canopy, dressed as Venus, being fanned by boy toys dressed as Cupid. It worked. Together they drank, shagged and laughed the days away, and six months after he finally said goodbye, she gave birth to a pair of twins who looked oddly Roman. Mark Antony eventually came running back, they got married, she popped out another son and they declared themselves gods, infuriating all of Rome. War broke out, drama ensued, she sent word she had died, he tried to kill himself, she said she was kidding, he returned and died in her arms, and so she killed herself with the help of a poisonous snake on her golden bed. It doesn't get any better than that.

TIBERIUS (42 B.C.–A.D. 37)

Adopted by his stepfather, the emperor Augustus, Tiberius led an unusually long and debauched life, reigning over Rome as the second emperor for the last twenty-three years of his life. Scholars claim that he started off well—he improved civil services, ran a tight ship and managed the finances of the state well enough— but somewhere along the line something snapped. He quickly gained a reputation as an absolute tyrant who enjoyed slaughtering innocents and offing the occasional family member, but it wasn't until he went into self-imposed exile on the Isle of Capri during his later years that his truly twisted nature fully emerged. In between entertainments at his pleasure palace—such as watching his enemies being thrown over the cliffs—his favorite pastime involved the large number of young boys and girls he had procured from around the Empire for his sexual amusement. While lolling about in the pool, his favorite delight was said to have been a group of young boys he called his "minnows" who darted about him in the water nibbling at his personals in a most un–PC manner. Regardless of whether the legends are true or exaggerated, Tiberius has secured his spot in history as one of the most twisted and creepy emperors of all time.

CALIGULA (A.D. 12–A.D. 41)

The third grandson of Tiberius, and the only one to escape his wrath alive, was born Gaius Caesar Augustus Germanicus. He was given the quaint nickname Caligula (meaning "Little Boots") by the soldiers in his father's army because of the military boots he sported as a child. He became emperor upon Tiberius's death, and though the masses were initially thrilled, they quickly learned that he was a madman of the first order. His absolute relish of torture and murder made his grandfather seem tame by comparison, and his most passionate love affair was with his own sister, Drusilla. But again, why judge? He proclaimed himself a god, threw some of the most

debauched dinner/orgies of all time, regularly bedded
the wives of his dinner guests and then humiliated them
all by recounting the details. At the height of his
madness, he tried to have his horse made a consul, and
within four years, crazy Little Boots was assassinated by
officers of his own guard. The little darling was eventually portrayed by Malcom McDowell in a god-awful film,
not to be missed, produced by the famed pornographer
Bob Guccione.

LOUIS XIV (1638–1715)

The seventy-two-year reign of France's self-proclaimed
"Sun King" was the longest in European history, and it
was marked by some of the greatest excesses ever seen.
The supremely narcissistic ruler not only indulged his
own vanity by donning six-inch heels, kabuki-style
makeup, hideously overwrought outfits and powdered
wigs, but in 1682 he moved the royal court to Versailles,
one of the most opulent palaces the world has ever seen.
Louis indulged his ego even further as he placed himself
at the very center of the splendor and watched as those
around him competed for his favor. Doling out gifts and
promises like bonbons to children, the king played the
members of his court and the guests he entertained like
a legion of marionettes. He even went so far as to invite
guests to watch him as he lived out his glorious daily routine, up to and including the depositing of his royal
coconuts in the toilet. His unending love of the splendor
and beauty of his own existence was matched only by his

insatiable need for continuous, intoxicating flattery, which he found in the loving arms of his countless mistresses.

CATHERINE THE GREAT (1762–1796)

Married to the idiotic man-child known as Peter III, the German princess Catherine endured nearly a decade-long sexless marriage before she decided to realize her royal position fully. With the swift precision of a master politician, she forced her husband to abdicate the throne and then had him quietly snuffed out just a few days later. She then proceeded to assume the throne of Russia and reigned for an amazing thirty-four years. During her reign she did much to bring culture, art, science and sophistication to her backward nation, and as a reward to herself, she embarked on an epic endeavor to satisfy her personal lust for hunky, young Adonises. Desperately romantic, she wrote flowery letters of longing to her lovers, but always seemed to bounce back in a hurry when the relationship suddenly headed south. With the demise of each subsequent affair, new prospects for the continuous parade were screened and selected by her ladies-in-waiting, or even by her favorite ex-lovers. One after the other, her *paramours du jour* were installed in an official apartment near her chambers and were regularly summoned to service her until she became bored with them or they broke her heart. Then they were sent packing with a generous "settlement." For a woman of her day, Catherine was exquisitely bold and unapologetic in her quest for satisfaction, and though the queen did love horses, there is no truth to those nasty rumors.

GEORGE IV (1762–1830)

Before he ascended to the British throne in 1820, when he was still the Prince of Wales, young George was a bon vivant of his day: young, handsome and outgoing despite being raised by a tyrannical and mad father. He quickly became known, however, for his increasingly obnoxious behavior and reckless spending. In 1811, he was bedridden for a time due to a twisted ankle he sustained while merrily dancing the highland fling. It was during this stressful convalescence, which was accompanied by the teensiest of nervous breakdowns, that he first developed a dependency on laudanum, a medicinal potion of the day made from opium, herbs and sherry wine. His prior reputation as a drunken gambler and womanizer had not endeared him to members of the royal court, the public or his wife, Caroline, who had a few issues and several love affairs of her own. Though he recovered from his emotional duress, his dependency on both opium and alcohol steadily increased to the point where he was barely coherent as a regent and often had to take up to 100 drops of laudanum before being able to face his governing duties. By the time he died, just seven years into his reign, he had become a gluttonous parody of his former self and an object of ridicule in the eyes of the public.

KING LUDWIG II (1845–1886)

Alternately known as "Mad King Ludwig," the "Swan King" or "The Dream King," Ludwig II of Bavaria staked his claim in the annals of history when he ascended the throne at the age of eighteen and embarked on a person-

"I like pigs. Dogs look up to us. Cats look down on us. Pigs treat us as equals."
—*Sir Winston Churchill*

WE ARE NOT STONED

Queen Victoria, the most upright and uptight of British monarchs, is reported to have used cannabis on a regular basis, as prescribed by her doctor, to relieve the royal menstrual discomforts.

al quest to turn his romantic fantasies into reality. Despite his tendency to remain in bed until the early evening—when he often washed down his breakfast with a bucketload of fine wine—Ludwig did manage to see his visions realized in the form of three fairy-tale castles he had built, complete with underground grottos and hidden swan boats for his personal entertaining. But it was Ludwig's uniquely charitable indulgences that set him apart. He loved nothing more than heading out under the cover of night in his horse-drawn sleigh, covered in ermine blankets with plumes of peacock feathers jutting from the back of the sleigh, to pay surprise visits to the local townspeople on whom he would bestow gifts of jewels and coins. Another of Ludwig's little hobbies became increasingly evident over time as soldiers leaving their horses at the royal stables noticed that several of the more attractive stable boys were always sporting sizable pieces of jewelry encrusted with precious gems. Eventually, the powers that were conspired to topple Ludwig, and just days after being declared insane and sequestered in one of his own castles, Ludwig drowned under mysterious circumstances in Lake Starnberg.

A TIMELINE OF INTOXICATION

Long before the hippies of the 1960s discovered their psychedelic wonderland, people across the globe had embarked upon a united quest for a good buzz, the expansion of consciousness and ultimate bliss. Since the dawn of time, the lure of serious pleasure has piqued both the curiosity and the enterprising nature of mankind.

C. 5000 B.C. Somewhere in the mountains between the Black and the Caspian Seas in what is today Armenia, the cultivation of grapes for winemaking begins.

C. 3400 B.C. Enterprising Mesopotamians with a little free time on their hands begin to cultivate the opium poppy, eventually passing along their discovery to the Babylonians and the Egyptians.

C. 3000 B.C. Native populations of South America discover the pleasure of chewing coca leaves and tell their neighbors with great enthusiasm.

C. 2500 B.C. Shipping and international trade in the Mediterranean Sea make wine production and export a profitable business. The drunken sailor is born.

C. 1400 Inca tribes in Peru begin cultivating coca in organized plantations and soon discover that consumption results in increased work productivity.

C. 1300 B.C. The opium trade expands in Egypt under the reign of the party-boy King Tutankhamen.

FIZZY BUZZY

By the late nineteenth century, "medicinal" cocaine was being used in everything from nasal sprays to cough drops, and in 1886, Coca-Cola was introduced as an energizing soft drink. The recipe contained cocaine-laced syrup, caffeine and flavorings from the kola nut. In 1901, cocaine was removed from the formula, leaving only traces. But it wasn't entirely removed until 1929, fifteen years after the United States had banned cocaine.

C. 330 B.C. Alexander the Great cements his popularity by introducing opium to the people of India and Persia.

70 Emperor Nero's physician makes mention of cannabis and its medicinal properties in his writings. Nero is too drunk to care.

1271 Explorer Marco Polo brings hashish to the attention of Europeans by writing of his exotic journeys and the wacky traditions of the "natives."

1516 The German Beer Purity Law is enacted, dictating that beer may only be made from barley, hops and pure water. It is an early sign of meticulous German engineering.

1632 The pilgrims bring hemp to New England as a sensible crop with multiple uses.

1650 The Dutch invent gin, a distilled liquor flavored with botanicals, spices, herbs and fruits. The English soon jump on it.

1791 Thomas Jefferson urges U.S. farmers to grow cannabis instead of tobacco.

1793 After years of exporting huge amounts to China, Britain's East India Company establishes a complete monopoly on the opium trade.

1802 Thomas Jefferson repeals the "Whiskey Tax," which he considers to be a hostile affront to decent people.

1805 The main active ingredient of the opium poppy, morphine, is purified.

1827 In Germany, E. Merck & Company is the first to manufacture morphine for commercial purposes. Soon, it will become the painkiller of choice for many years.

1843 British physician Dr. Alexander Wood, a master of efficiency, is the first to inject morphine through a syringe.

1884 Viennese egghead Sigmund Freud embarks on a shameless quest for publicity by extolling the medicinal and psychological benefits of cocaine, which he himself enjoys. He later recants when things get a bit messy.

1890 The U.S. government imposes a tax on morphine and opium as recreational use spreads.

1909 An international conference on opium is initiated by President Theodore Roosevelt and held in Shanghai to address the perils of the opium trade.

1915 The Harrison Narcotics Act becomes law in the United States. Originally intended to regulate the prescription, distribution and taxation of opium, cocaine and other narcotics, it soon becomes a law of prohibition.

1920 The 18th Amendment goes into effect in the United States, and prohibition becomes the law of the land, forbidding the manufacture, sale, transportation, import or export of alcoholic beverages. But without widespread public support, organized crime takes over and the Roaring '20s begin.

1933 Prohibition is repealed as the 21st Amendment goes into effect, and the party is back on.

1973 President Richard Nixon creates the Drug Enforcement Administration, giving a single agency all federal powers of drug enforcement.

1978 U.S. and Mexican officials try to combat opium production by spraying opium fields with Agent Orange. To their utter surprise, production of opium increases in Pakistan, Afghanistan and Iran.

1978 The first coffee shop licensed to sell cannabis opens in Amsterdam.

1984 Ecstasy first becomes popular in the United States in the unlikely setting of the dance clubs of Dallas and Austin, Texas.

2002 U.N. Drug Control and Crime Prevention Agency names Afghanistan as the world's largest producer of opium.

2004 The British government downgrades cannabis to the category including steroids and antidepressants, and possession is no longer cause for arrest, with a few exceptions. Keith Richards doesn't notice.

THE PURITANS — THE LOUSIEST DINNER GUESTS EVER

One of the more unfortunate lingering influences in the collective psyche of America can be traced back to the country's very origin. Though the Puritans were rebelling in a big way when they left England in protest against the British monarchy and the Church of England, theirs was a religious rebellion, and as rebellions go, religious ones are not particularly sexy. They brought to the colonies a dreary collection of beliefs that, amazingly, still informs the morals of many of the nation's more conservative types.

The Puritans steadfastly believed in a literal interpretation of the Scriptures, and they maintained that an austere and disciplined life was a pure life. They frowned upon excess of any kind and believed in simple clothing for priests, simple ceremonies and the simplest decoration in their churches. This is ironic since they were so very committed to recruiting new members to their churches. Take away the flashy costumes and gaudy windows, and you've lost a good deal of the entertainment value of organized religion. And yet they persisted.

They espoused the virtues of disciplined study, hard work and high standards of moral excellence. They frowned upon idleness and encouraged that most tedious of qualities, thrift. They did contribute some valuable ideas to the evolving democracy, and though

they believed strongly in the separation of church and
state, they were terribly intolerant of other beliefs,
and had no sense of fun whatsoever when it came to
witches. One would think that in the bleak days of early
colonial living a little magic would be a nice diversion,
but no. Wizardry and superstition were strictly verboten
for these dully-draped stiffs. And given their tendency to
ramble on about their religion at all hours, their candlelight suppers for their Native American friends probably
weren't the lusty bacchanals one might expect when an
exotic new set of friends bearing peace pipes shows up.

However, despite their rigid belief systems, even the
Puritans could not rise above their all-too-human incli-
nation to seek the warm and fuzzy glow that can only be
found through a good stiff drink. Contrary to popular
opinion, the Puritans were not immune to the pleasures
of alcohol. Of course, they thoroughly disapproved of
drunkenness and more than a few messy Marys were
thrown into the stockades, but it is said that upon setting
sail for the colonies, the Puritans loaded more beer than
drinking water onto the Mayflower. They made booze
out of everything they could find, from squash to beets,
and they even let the kids have the occasional tipple in
the name of disease prevention, as the poor quality of the
well water brought its own set of hazards to the young.

Additionally, the Puritans were perfectly happy to use
liquor in their bartering with the Indians, and the international rum trade quickly became one of the most prof-

> "We must learn to distinguish morality from moralizing."
> —Henry Kissinger

itable ventures in the New World. So, even in the earliest days, we can see that the pleasures and profitability of vice can never be fully denied. And yet there are still plenty of righteous souls today who rant against the evils of pleasure and hedonism. These are the people who are in steep denial of human nature, and their tendencies to pass judgment on others only reflect the inner torment and fear they harbor, the weakness they feel when faced with their own temptations. That is, until they are videotaped in a hotel room with a hooker and a bag of coke, at which point they tearfully confess their own vulnerability, and suddenly it's all about forgiveness.

TOP TEN HEDONIST MANTRAS

A cliché can only become a cliché if it is in some way rooted in truth. And regardless of their origins, certain truisms and rallying cries cannot be denied. Herewith, let us review some of the essential phrases that regularly float through the mind of the practical hedonist:

"CARPE DIEM!"

1. LIVE AND LET LIVE.

*

2. CARPE DIEM.

*

3. YOU CAN'T TAKE IT WITH YOU.

*

4. 'TIS BETTER TO HAVE LIVED.

*

5. SHIT OR GET OFF THE POT.

6. YOU ONLY LIVE ONCE.

*

7. JUST DO IT.

*

8. I'M TOO SEXY.

*

9. NEVER SAY NEVER.

*

10. HAS ANYBODY SEEN MY KEYS?

It is possible that not all of these mantras have passed the lips of history's towering figures of excess, but linguistics and modern vernacular aside, they all surely murmured something along those lines at some point in the game. Why? Because history may change many things, but the essence of life has remained the same since the beginning of time. It is a journey, and everyone must make time to examine exactly where their journey is leading them.

Where Is My Life?

II

"ONE OF THE SYMPTOMS OF AN APPROACHING NERVOUS BREAKDOWN IS THE BELIEF THAT ONE'S WORK IS TERRIBLY IMPORTANT."

— Bertrand Russell

SO HISTORY IS FULL OF DEBAUCHED SLOPPIES WHO DRANK, drugged and buggered their way through life, sometimes to tragic ends. Are these to be taken as examples of the good life? Hardly. As always, the pendulum swings, and the excessive, unrestrained indulgences of our forebears simply represent the dangers of unbridled hedonism. A touch of restraint and self-control would have behooved these messy characters immeasurably, and from their examples we can see the necessity of balance and practicality.

But now it seems the pendulum has swung to the other side of the continuum in a big way. Over time, and very surreptitiously, the modern masses have been indoctrinated into a mindset in which no amount of work, money, success or achievement is ever enough. Step off the treadmill and you will fall irretrievably behind. Sit down to watch the sunset and opportunity may escape you. The once ironic term "workaholic" is now applicable to an alarming number of people, all of whom believe that they simply have no choice in the matter.

This is, of course, untrue. One of the inherent rights that comes with incarnation in this world is free will. Will the business really fall apart if you stop micromanaging? Will the household really implode if you stop cooking, cleaning and providing? Will your lover really lose his mittens and wander into the traffic if you're not there to remind and second-guess every step of the way? No. And to prove this fact, all you need to do is die. What would happen then? Things would work themselves out, that's what.

The bottom line here is that you are not your job. Or at least you shouldn't be. You are not a to-do list, a series of responsibilities or a roster of achievements. Your life consists of much more than that, and your foremost responsibility is to yourself (unless of course you have very small children, in which case your nirvana may be temporarily compromised). By ensuring your own happiness and enjoying your own life to whatever degree is reasonable, you will better be able to share your happiness and infectious joy with those around you. Embracing pleasure is not selfish, it is the height of selflessness.

So how does your life measure up on the scale of duty vs. pleasure? Are joy, indulgence and leisure high on your list of priorities, or are you living in a horrid little spider hole of cyber-addiction, work-related obligations and odious selflessness?

TOP TEN SIGNS YOU'RE IN TOO DEEP

If five or more of the following signs are true for you, you may be in need of a hedonistic intervention. It is advised that you immediately turn off all electronic devices and lie down.

1. YOU NO LONGER REMEMBER ANYONE'S PHONE NUMBER BECAUSE THEY'RE ALL PROGRAMMED INTO YOUR CELL PHONE.

2. YOU INSTANT MESSAGE PEOPLE AT WORK WHO ARE SEATED WITHIN TWENTY FEET OF YOU.

3. YOU MAKE ITINERARIES FOR YOUR VACATIONS.

*

4. THE IDEA OF A FULL WEEK WITHOUT INTERNET ACCESS
FILLS YOU WITH TERROR.

*

5. YOU ARE BORED AT HOME IF THE TELEVISION ISN'T ON.

*

6. YOU ABSOLUTELY MUST WATCH THE NEWS EVERY DAY
TO BE SURE THE WORLD ISN'T ENDING.

*

7. YOU REGULARLY WATCH SITCOM RERUNS THAT YOU
HAVE SEEN COUNTLESS TIMES BEFORE.

*

8. YOU ARE UNABLE TO SIT STILL AND THINK IN SILENCE.

*

9. YOUR CONVERSATION REGULARLY REVOLVES AROUND
THE LIVES OF OTHERS INSTEAD OF YOUR OWN.

*

10. YOU BUY SHOES BECAUSE THEY MATCH YOUR IPOD.

WORK LESS, ACHIEVE MORE

The oft-praised principles of hard work, driving ambition and the quest to win are to be avoided at all costs, not only because they are unnecessarily exhausting, but also because they are ineffective. For those trying to push and shove their way to the top, the advice is simple: Knock it off.

Greed, ego, selfishness and the desire to gain power over others are often the underlying motivating factors behind unbridled ambition, and any endeavor fueled by such ugliness will always result in ultimate defeat. It is far better to expend one's energies in a positive spirit of assumed ease and no resistance. If you focus on the work that truly matters and try to enjoy the process, things will go much more smoothly and success will come much more quickly.

If your work is hard, you need to find ways to make it easier. If you're doing too much, you need to take stock and determine what is unnecessary. The belief that only hard work is worthwhile is completely absurd. Any work can be made "hard." Planting a fern can be difficult if you decide that blueprints and plans are required, make a spreadsheet listing the tools you'll need, schedule the planting and run soil tests before you begin. Just stick the thing in the ground and get out of the way.

> "Any fool can make things bigger, more complex, and more violent. It takes a touch of genius—and a lot of courage— to move in the opposite direction."
> —*Albert Einstein*

In Vedic science, an ancient Indian philosophy, it is known as "economy of effort." You will achieve far better results by simply applying your energies only toward those things that are essential. Anything more is wasted effort and only heightens the possibility of complication.

Of course, in the eyes of a true control freak, this may seem like little more than an excuse for laziness, but that is an entirely inaccurate assessment. It is the efficient application of resources that gets the job done with the greatest of ease in the shortest time possible. No stress, no fuss, no problem, and there's time left over for a nice long lunch.

Energy is a valuable commodity not to be wasted on futile pursuits or neurotic obsessions when it could and should be applied to the cultivation of love, happiness and pleasure. Far too many people apply their energies to the convoluted maintenance of their own egos and their own sense of self-importance. "The longer the list of duties, tasks, obligations and responsibilities I have, the more important I am. And the more important I am, the longer my list of duties, tasks, obligations and responsibilities." Yawn. If those same energies could be freed up, they could be applied to far more noble and rewarding pursuits, and those misguided souls who are chasing their own tails and insisting that everyone else do the same would be a lot more tolerable.

TEN SENSIBLE RULES FOR THE WORKPLACE

1. ALWAYS TAKE THE PATH OF LEAST RESISTANCE.

2. NEVER DO MORE THAN IS TRULY NECESSARY.

3. KNOW YOUR INTENTION AND FOCUS ON THE GOAL.

4. TAKE RESPONSIBILITY ONLY FOR THAT WHICH IS YOURS.

5. ACCEPT THAT YOU CAN CONTROL ONLY YOUR OWN ACTIONS.

6. DO NOT ATTEMPT TO CONTROL OTHERS.

7. ALWAYS REMAIN FLEXIBLE.

8. IF IT'S A STRUGGLE, RETHINK IT.

9. NEVER TRY TO FORCE A SITUATION.

10. KEEP IT IN PERSPECTIVE.

"NEVER TRY TO FORCE A SITUATION."

TIME OFF? HAHAHAHAHA!

Back in the '80s, U.S. workers used to giggle and point at the manic pace of the Japanese work force. Oh, those poor people, entirely unaware of life's pleasures, racing to make a yen and take over the world economy. But since those days of big money and big hair, a karmic tsunami of sorts has turned the tables, and Americans now find themselves working longer hours than the people of any other nation on earth. As they scurry off to work, they race past relaxed tourists from other nations leisurely strolling about their cities, cameras in hand, trying to decide between lunch or one more amusing diversion.

As the national economy began to wobble and the job market became more competitive, forty-hour work weeks extended to fifty or more, people began taking on second or even third jobs, and suddenly everyone was exhausted to the point of complete and utter numbness. For many, the mere idea of a vacation became an unattainable dream, and if that dream were to be realized, it would mean time off without pay. For those who were granted actual paid vacations, time off became little more than a suspension of aggravation. A week away from work only meant a backlog of a week's worth of work, and wouldn't it just be easier to work through and avoid the inevitable scramble to catch up?

Such a predicament is both preposterous and inhumane. When the job becomes so all-consuming that leisure becomes a shrinking dream, something is very wrong. And at that point, one must look to one's government and the quality of life it ensures for its citizens. In most industrialized nations, law requires that a minimum of vacation days be allotted to all workers, regardless of their profession. According to a 2002 study by the European Industrial Relations Observatory, these are the statutory minimum periods of paid annual leave in various countries:

"With virtue and quietness one may conquer the world."
—*Lao-Tzu*

TOP TEN REASONS BIG
RATS ABANDON THE RACE

☞ Burnout

☞ Revelation

☞ The arrival of children

☞ Bankruptcy

☞ True love

☞ Tedious lawsuits

☞ Life-threatening disease

☞ Downsizing

☞ Scandal

☞ Rehab

COUNTRY	PAID VACATION DAYS REQUIRED BY LAW
SWEDEN	25
AUSTRIA	25
DENMARK	25
SPAIN	25
FRANCE	25
GERMANY	24
FINLAND	24
PORTUGAL	22
NORWAY	21
ITALY	20
SWITZERLAND	20
IRELAND	20
AUSTRALIA	20
NETHERLANDS	20
UNITED KINGDOM	20
BELGIUM	20
GREECE	20
CHINA	15
JAPAN	10
UNITED STATES*	0

(Though there is no national vacation requirement in the United States, some requirements do exist for public employees.)

STRESS INDEED

Feelings of stress are more than just emotional perception. When the mind believes that danger is present, the old biological fight-or-flight impulse kicks in. Of course, the impulse originally evolved in the human psyche to provide the physical energy boost required to flee from a lion or to fight off a sword-wielding Hun from over the hill. When the impulse is triggered, the heart rate rises, blood pressure soars and blood flows from the stomach to the arms, the legs and the brain so that great physical challenges can be met. But if all this is repeatedly happening while you're sitting in traffic or stewing at your desk with no physical outlet, it's like regularly blasting the stereo at top volume for no reason. Eventually, you're going to blow a speaker.

Stress is real, and it is a direct result of your perceptions about what is happening around you. If you allow yourself to get worked up into a frenzy on a regular basis, and then keep it all bottled up inside, you will actually be causing yourself physical harm. And since emotional outbursts are frowned upon in the workplace, a brisk walk around the block or a quick set of squats in the bathroom stall may be in order as you calmly remind yourself, "There is no lion. There is no lion."

Stress is neither a symbol of status nor an indication of your importance, it is merely a one-way ticket to high blood pressure, jangled nerves, physical exhaustion,

SENSIBLE WEEKLY TIME ALLOCATION

WORK
40 hours (It's the law!)

SLEEP
56 hours (Eight hours per night.)

CHORES
6 hours (Necessary evil, delegate when possible.)

LEISURE
66 hours (Use them well.)

emotional instability or even a heart attack. These are not pleasurable things, and therefore, at all times, stress should be avoided as if it were the plague.

A NOTE TO THE WORKERS

ACCORDING TO THE AMERICAN PSYCHOLOGICAL ASSOCIATION:

43 PERCENT OF ADULTS SUFFER ADVERSE HEALTH EFFECTS FROM STRESS.

75–90 PERCENT OF ALL PHYSICIAN OFFICE VISITS ARE FOR STRESS-RELATED AILMENTS AND COMPLAINTS.

STRESS IS LINKED TO THE SIX LEADING CAUSES OF DEATH: HEART DISEASE, CANCER, LUNG AILMENTS, ACCIDENTS, CIRRHOSIS OF THE LIVER AND SUICIDE.

A NOTE TO MANAGEMENT

ACCORDING TO THE AMERICAN PSYCHOLOGICAL ASSOCIATION:

IN TERMS OF LOST HOURS DUE TO ABSENTEEISM, REDUCED PRODUCTIVITY AND WORKER COMPENSATION BENEFITS, STRESS COSTS AMERICAN INDUSTRY MORE THAN $300 BILLION ANNUALLY.

UNPLUG

The idea of unplugging is essential in today's high-tech, manic world of continuous stimulation if one is to truly embrace the concepts of leisure and pleasure. Downing a bottle of wine as you surf the Internet just won't cut it. Not only must one unplug from the cell phone, the laptop and the Palm Pilot, but also from work, drama and responsibility.

Though the Dalai Lama may have Internet access, he and his most ardent followers have always known that true bliss is best achieved through silence, meditation and complete stillness. That's not to say that achieving such a state automatically brings on some magical buzz of euphoria, but rather that the complete absence of thought, ego, stress, noise and action allows the being in question to simply exist in perfect harmony with the universe. Of course, only a select few are able to achieve such cosmic stillness through the discipline of medita-tion. Most people find it much easier to attain that same state with the assistance of select chemicals. But re-gardless of the means, the quest for inner peace and emotional tranquility is an all-too-human impulse, and a very noble one at that.

"Remember that the most beautiful things in life are the most useless; peacocks and lilies, for example."
—*John Ruskin*

Einstein proved long ago that time is a relative concept—it can expand and contract—and it is entirely possible to adjust the pace of one's life by simply slowing down. In today's frenzied climate, silence, stillness and tran-quility have become decadent luxuries. Happily, they are luxuries available to all, regardless of budget.

TEN SURE-FIRE WAYS TO SLOW TIME DOWN

"EXTEND FOREPLAY."

Simple and obvious, you say? Well, of course they are. But by experimenting with these painfully simple procedures, you will be embarking on your higher journey by taking the proverbial first steps toward unleashing your inner hedonist.

1. FIND A PARK BENCH, SIT AND OBSERVE LIFE.

2. LIE IN A HAMMOCK AND STARE AT THE STARS.

3. BOB IN THE OCEAN.

4. GO FOR A WALK WITHOUT DIRECTION.

5. READ A BOOK IN COMPLETE SILENCE.

6. TAKE A NAP IN THE SUN.

7. TAKE A BATH BY CANDLELIGHT.

8. SLEEP UNTIL YOU CAN SLEEP NO MORE.

9. EXTEND FOREPLAY.

10. WATCH SWEDISH CINEMA.

REALITY TELEVISION — THE SADDEST OF ADDICTIONS

Teenagers belting out show tunes at the top of their lungs. Postal workers wearing puka shells while running obstacle courses in the tropics. Underwear models hanging suspended from helicopters while eating worms. Have such displays insinuated their way into your weekly routine? Do you find yourself parked on the couch accepting the staged "realities" of other people's lives as entertainment? If so, you are in desperate need of a little action of your own.

There is no denying that such television programming is heinously addictive, and it must be acknowledged that there is something inherently entertaining about watching others subject themselves to public humiliation. Most people who watch beauty pageants do not do so in hopes of discovering the true meaning of beauty, but rather in hopes that Miss South Carolina will say something truly idiotic or trip on her evening gown and tumble down the stairs. Figure skating garners huge TV ratings not because a triple salchow (yes, that's how you spell it, thank you very much) sets the spirit free, but because there are very few opportunities in life to see someone clad in sequins fall on her ass. We love it when others fail.

> "Time has convinced me of one thing: Television is for appearing on—not for looking at."
> —*Noel Coward*

But these are shallow pleasures, unworthy of a true hedonist. And an addiction to such manipulative drivel is a sign that you are short a few sequins in your own life. In small doses, such entertainments should not be begrudged, but if you haven't fallen on your own ass in the last year, either literally or figuratively, a little self-examination is in order. When was the last time you took a risk? Where are your thrills? When was the last time you set foot on an island, let alone got booted off? It's easy to laugh and feel superior to those who are chasing silly dreams, but a silly dream is better than no dream at all.

KILL THE TELEVISION — THE
ULTIMATE BRAIN WORKOUT

At this point, we venture into tricky territory. "Is it not pleasurable to recline, watching television, chips-on-belly, letting the mind float freely?" you may ask. Well, yes, that argument could probably be supported, but that is not what Epicurus and his fellow philosophers had in mind when they examined the purpose of a life well led. The idea was that the human spirit seeks out that which is pleasurable. Notice the presence of the verb—seek.

Though it may seem contradictory, action is required in the pursuit of pleasure. You must *climb* into the hammock. You must *pour* the wine. And you must *create* a life that is both engaging and pleasurable, not just easy. The determining factor is whether you are enjoying your own life or enjoying the lives of others. True hedonism involves experience. And though watching can in itself be lots of fun, it is not so much hedonism as voyeurism. And if you are truly committed to the pleasures of voyeurism, you should be using binoculars rather than a television set.

THE PERILS OF STRUCTURED LIVING

Numerous are the consequences of living an overly structured and disciplined life. To deny leisure and pleasure their due respect is to spit in the face of the true meaning of life. If you are among the many who have drifted from the true path, you must be prepared to pay a hefty price indeed. Here are but a few of the unpleasant side effects in store for you:

YOU WILL BE UNPOPULAR AT PARTIES.

YOU WILL BECOME HARDENED AND BITTER.

YOU WILL AGE PREMATURELY.

YOU WILL EXPERIENCE GREATER STRESS.
YOUR RELATIONSHIPS WILL SUFFER.

YOU WILL SPEND YOUR LIFE STRUGGLING.

YOU WILL FEEL CHEATED.

YOU WILL FEEL LEFT OUT.

YOU WILL HAVE SERIOUS REGRETS IN THE END.

YOU WILL NOT BE HAPPY.

If any of the consequences listed above have an uncomfortably familiar ring to them, you need not panic. Your hedonistic muscles may have atrophied slightly, but they are still there just waiting for a vigorous workout. An abrupt 180-degree turnaround is probably not advisable at this point, but the first step on the road to your personal rehabilitation must be a reevaluation of your belief system. As the snake sheds its skin, so must you shed the uncomfortable and restricting cloak of misguided values that has slowly and surreptitiously enveloped you.

Overrated Virtues

III

"IT HAS BEEN MY EXPERIENCE THAT FOLKS WHO
HAVE NO VICES HAVE VERY FEW VIRTUES."

— Abraham Lincoln

IT'S GOOD TO BE BAD

AS HONEST ABE POINTS OUT, MOST OF US ARE GOOD SOME OF the time, and some of us are good most of the time, but any one of us who claims to be good all of the time is an asshole. This has been proven time and time again as sobbing televangelists, defrocked priests and disgraced moralists have been paraded across the television screen, being led by the elbows into the hallowed halls of justice. It's a beautiful thing, that.

In the grand gallery of human characters, one of the most irritating archetypes is the always-annoying Pollyanna. Perky and chirpy, always smiling and perpetually well behaved is no way to go through life—at least not if you want to have friends. Human nature is both complicated and multidimensional, and to live in denial of the dark side is not only pointless and unnecessarily restrictive, it can also lead to personal ruin. As an evolving growth process, life must be fully embraced in order for it to have any meaning whatsoever.

Centuries of religious dogma and puritanical residue have soiled the good name of the dark side. Darkness and evil are not the same thing. Virtually every child is told at some point not to be afraid of the dark. There is nothing there in the dark that doesn't exist in the light, and hence there is no reason to feel threatened. However, once this comforting reassurance is solidly in place, the rug is promptly pulled from beneath us. A barrage of dire warnings is unleashed upon the fragile mind by society at large. Beware of the dark side, we are told, as if all of life's evils are lurking in one location. It's a curious reversal of logic, and a puzzling mystery indeed.

There can be no light without darkness, and neither realm has exclusive dibs on that which is good or bad. After all, violence, aggression and hostility are perfectly happy to rear their ugly heads in broad daylight. There is great beauty to be found in the dimly lit recesses of the soul, and at its best, darkness can be romantic, inspiring, exhilarating, fascinating and eye-opening. To deny its allure is to reject half of the life experience. To fearlessly enjoy the full spectrum of human nature is not only wise, it is logical, and any goody-two-shoes who claims to be of superior virtue and immune to temptation should be met with instantaneous suspicion. It is entirely unnatural to be "good" all the time, especially since "goodness" is often a prescribed recipe of someone else's design. The truth is that a little bit of bad is a very good thing.

> "Few things are harder to put up with than the annoyance of a good example."
> —*Mark Twain*

DECEPTIVE VIRTUES OF WORLD LEADERS

The age-old debate over the importance of virtue in both the personal and political realm has heated up considerably in the past few decades. In today's media-saturated, scandal-hungry environment, anyone foolish enough to seek public office knows that his or her life will be dissected down to the most minute detail. Detractors will scratch and claw in the dark corners of the past, searching for an incident, a comment or even a single photograph that can be used to discredit the candidate in question.

Character assassination has become public sport, and sadly, a person's entire career can be potentially destroyed by a youthful indiscretion, a comment taken out of context or an innocent sex tape shot through night-vision goggles. It's certainly taken a lot of the fun out of politics. But on the flipside, the public has become more forgiving. Certainly, celebrities are given greater leeway on the scales of scandal. In fact, scandals often launch a career rather than destroy it these days, but American politicians are still being held to ridiculous standards.

When France's former president, François Mitterand, died in 1996, both his wife and his longtime mistress attended the state funeral, maintaining their composure and dignity throughout, and the French did not see it as anything particularly scandalous. Had such a situation occurred in the States, the shrieks of horror would have been deafening. This is largely because many Americans still insist on believing that things are what they appear to be. But in fact, things are rarely what they appear to be. And to assume that a person's true character can be accurately assessed by judging their personal behavior is hopelessly naïve.

A QUICK QUIZ

In recent years, a very telling little quiz has circulated the Internet. Though surely paraphrased, rewritten and approximate in detail, as Internet wisdom usually is, the point of the illustration is inescapably clear.

QUESTION:

It is time to elect a new world leader, and only your vote counts. You are presented with three candidates from which to choose, and you are given the following information regarding their characters. Which one do you choose?

CANDIDATE A   CANDIDATE B   CANDIDATE C

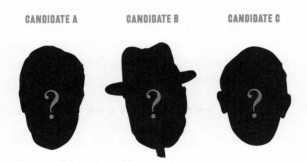

This man has been known to associate with crooked politicians and consult with astrologers. He's had two mistresses, he chain smokes and he drinks eight to ten martinis a day.

This man has been kicked out of office twice, regularly sleeps until noon, used opium in college and drinks a quart of whiskey every evening.

This man is a decorated war hero. He's also a vegetarian, he doesn't smoke, drinks only an occasional beer and never cheated on his wife.

WHICH CANDIDATE WOULD YOU CHOOSE?

CANDIDATE A
is Franklin D. Roosevelt.

CANDIDATE B
is Winston Churchill.

CANDIDATE C
is Adolf Hitler.

You see? In the grand social laboratory of life, we can clearly and safely conclude that a "clean" life is hardly a barometer of worthiness, let alone the absence of evil. Wisdom, vision and leadership are not the products of sobriety and "moral" rectitude, but inherent qualities that cannot be extinguished by a little bender or a casual fling now and then.

FOR THE RECORD — LOONEY LAWS

As the tides of political progress ebb and flow with archaic conventions crashing like waves on the shore, and with political steps forward receding just as regularly due to the ever-present undertow of the right wing, the modern hedonist must always navigate the surf with caution. Though the urge to rebel may be healthy and productive, it can also be exhausting and unnecessary at times. One must choose one's battles wisely in order to have the greatest effect. Sometimes it's best to just sit on the sidelines with a bowl of popcorn, watch the show and laugh.

BARSTOOL WISDOM

The first draft of the Declaration of Independence was written by Thomas Jefferson not in some handsomely appointed library or office, but in a Philadelphia tavern.

Nothing pleases the powers that be more than a population of lemmings. Those who follow obediently make the best workers and the best citizens because they are easily manipulated and rarely question authority. Deny them anything and they will accept it. Then there are those who question absolutely everything and rage against the machine endlessly. Both groups are equally irritating. For the sane majority, the importance of law is understood, but it is equally important to recognize that as society evolves, so must the laws of the land. This most basic of principles was eloquently explained and is literally carved in stone at the Jefferson Memorial in Washington, D.C.

> I am not an advocate for frequent changes in laws and constitutions. But laws and institutions must go hand in hand with the progress of the human mind. As that becomes more developed, more enlightened, as new discoveries are made, new truths discovered and manners and opinions change, with the change of circumstances, institutions must advance also to keep pace with the times. We might as well require a man to wear still the coat which fitted him when a boy as civilized society to remain ever under the regimen of their barbarous ancestors.
>
> Thomas Jefferson.

Generally speaking, it's the broad laws that tend to remain unchallenged and unchanged. Murder, theft and kidnapping have pretty much been agreed upon—bad, very bad. But the laws that infringe upon civil liberties have always inspired debate and are constantly being amended and questioned. Prohibition was arguably the biggest legal failure of the twentieth century. The misguided effort to reduce crime, improve productivity and resolve social problems backfired in spectacular fashion as organized crime exploded, significant tax revenue was lost and alcohol consumption ultimately increased. By criminalizing the sale and consumption of alcoholic beverages, the government created a massive and very lucrative black market.

The current "war on drugs" is considered by many to be another misguided endeavor of epic proportions. It is simply not possible to eradicate the use of drugs. The Dutch government has provided a new model of effective drug law enforcement by regulating them as opposed to prohibiting them. In the Netherlands, drug users are not considered criminals. It is understood that drug use in itself does not lead to crime, but if the supply of drugs is deemed a criminal affair, then the user must resort to criminal behavior in order to access the supply of drugs. By decriminalizing the drug trade and regulating it, with responsible social programs in place to assist users in trouble, the government has effectively eliminated an entire category of crime. This in turn reduces the burdens on the legal system, the police force and the prison system. In fact, drug use in the Netherlands has declined and is now significantly lower than in many other European countries. Once the illicit nature of the drug is removed, the realities of drug taking come into focus, and people begin to act in a more responsible and sensible manner. Of course, then there are those giggling stoned tourists staggering out of the coffee shops, but is that really any different than the heavily tranquilized New York socialite weaving down Park Avenue after a visit to the doctor?

And speaking of New York, we can now examine a little collection of laws that are simply ludicrous. Under the reign of the emperor Michael Bloomberg, New York City has recently been deluged with a shocking number of strange, new and capricious laws. It seems the no-smoking laws were just the tip of the iceberg. It is now illegal in New York City to feed the pigeons, to sit on a milk crate, to ride a bicycle with one's feet off the pedals or to place a bag on an empty subway seat. And while the aforementioned smokers are now required to step outside for a cigarette break, they can be cited for loitering on a sidewalk in front of a business. Each of these hideous crimes can result in a stiff fine if the offender is unfortunate enough to have said crime witnessed by the police. It is in cases such as these that the public begins to wonder about the priorities of the politicians.

Though New Yorkers may be entirely unaware as they wantonly break the law on a daily basis, they are not the only ones in constant peril of acquiring sudden and unexpected criminal status:

IN ALASKA: No person may look at a moose from an airplane.

IN OHIO: It is illegal for a woman to wear patent leather shoes in public.

IN CALIFORNIA: A woman wearing a bathrobe may not operate a car.

IN MICHIGAN: It is illegal for a woman to cut her hair without her husband's permission.

IN FLORIDA: No one may have sexual relations with a porcupine.

IN ILLINOIS: Bathing is prohibited during the winter.

IN ARIZONA: No one may gargle in public.

IN NEW JERSEY: No horse racing is allowed on the turnpike.

IN MASSACHUSETTS: A husband and wife may not kiss in public on Sundays.

IN ALABAMA: It is illegal to play dominos on Sunday.

ACT 69

In 1913, Nebraska ruled that oral sex was illegal. In a supremely ironic twist, the law was the 69th piece of legislation to be passed that year, and thus became officially known as Act 69.

IN MAINE: You may not step out of a plane in flight.

IN INDIANA: It is illegal to make a monkey smoke a cigarette.

Is anybody having fun anymore?!?!

DISCIPLINE — FUTILE IN GOVERNMENT, FUN IN THE BEDROOM

Since time began, authorities have tried to convince the public to exercise self-discipline through every conceivable means, from intimidation and superstition to outright propaganda. But it wasn't until 1533, when King Henry VIII broke with the Catholic Church to establish the Church of England, that church doctrine became law and sodomy, loosely defined as any nonprocreative sex act, was deemed a criminal offense. When the Puritans established the American colonies, they carried over many of the laws of England and decided that sodomy was so unforgivable that it should carry the penalty of death.

Privacy rights have always inspired furious debate between those who believe that the sexual practices of consenting adults behind closed doors are a personal matter, and those who, for some inexplicable reason,

OH, IDAHO!

In 1971, Idaho became the first state to repeal its anti-sodomy law. Under hysterical pressure from the Mormon and Catholic Churches, the original laws were reinstated in 1972, making sodomy a felony once again.

THE MAINE EVENT

In 1955, Maine became the first state to rule that masturbating another person does not violate the state's anti-sodomy law.

believe it is their business to legislate the sex lives of others. But on June 26, 2003, the U.S. Supreme Court ruled in a 6–3 vote that sodomy laws were unconstitutional. Until that ruling was passed, nine states and the territory of Puerto Rico still had antisodomy laws that applied to both heterosexuals and homosexuals. Four states had antisodomy laws that only applied to homosexuals. Some were so strict that even a married couple could be arrested for engaging in oral sex in their own home.

TEXAS

MISDEMEANOR PUNISHABLE BY $500

Law applies only to same-sex couples and becomes the flashpoint that leads to the Supreme Court ruling of 2003

IDAHO

FELONY PUNISHABLE BY FIVE YEARS TO LIFE

Any sexual penetration is sufficient to complete the crime against nature.

HERE'S A SNAPSHOT OF THE NONPROCREATIVE SEX ACT SITUATION ON JUNE 25, 2003

UTAH

MISDEMEANOR PUNISHABLE BY $299/SIX MONTHS

Law pertains to any oral or anal sexual act, heterosexual or homosexual

OKLAHOMA

FELONY PUNISHABLE BY TEN YEARS

In 1986, the law was struck down as it applied to heterosexuals, but not homosexuals.

Despite the Supreme Court's recent decision, attempts to legislate the rights of individuals persist. The debate over gay marriage continues to polarize the country, and in the minds of many, the "pursuit of happiness" guaranteed by the Constitution does not apply to everyone. But as Thomas Jefferson pointed out, laws must change in accordance with the evolution of society. After all, as recently as 1967, sixteen states still prohibited interracial marriage.

MICHIGAN
FELONY PUNISHABLE
BY FIFTEEN YEARS

Any sexual penetration, however slight, shall be deemed sufficient to complete the crime.

MISSISSIPPI
FELONY PUNISHABLE
BY TEN YEARS

Applicable to any "detestable and abominable crimes" committed with mankind or with a beast

KANSAS
MISDEMEANOR PUNISHABLE
BY $1000/SIX MONTHS

Applicable only to lesbian or gay couples

VIRGINIA
FELONY PUNISHABLE
BY FIVE YEARS

Law pertains to any oral or anal sexual act regardless of sexual orientation

NORTH CAROLINA
FELONY PUNISHABLE
BY THREE YEARS

Applicable to any "crimes against nature, with mankind or beast"

ALABAMA
MISDEMEANOR PUNISHABLE
BY $2000/ONE YEAR

Does not apply to married couples

FLORIDA
MISDEMEANOR PUNISHABLE
BY $500/60 DAYS

Breast-feeding mothers deemed not unnatural or lascivious (very generous)

LOUISIANA
FELONY PUNISHABLE
BY $2000/FIVE YEARS

Defined as "unnatural carnal copulation" with another of the same or opposite sex, or with an animal, with the odd exemption of anal sex in certain circumstances

MISSOURI
MISDEMEANOR PUNISHABLE
BY $1000/ONE YEAR

Applies only to persons who have "deviate sexual intercourse with another person of the same sex"

SOUTH CAROLINA
FELONY PUNISHABLE
BY $500/FIVE YEARS

The state statute actually refers to the "abominable crime of buggery," applicable to both heterosexual and homosexual couples.

PUERTO RICO
FELONY PUNISHABLE
BY 8–20 YEARS

Anal sex is illegal between any two people, but oral sex is illegal only between same-sex couples.

THE SEVEN DEADLY SINS

Certainly laws are necessary in any civilized society, but because human beings in their natural states have always been selfish, nasty, debauched and shiftless, it was inevitable that a moral code of sorts would also be required to help the hapless masses classify their personality characteristics. The very notions of vice and virtue have been debated for eons, with everyone from Plato to a parade of popes weighing in on the subject. But by the Middle Ages, the Catholic Church had the list nailed down at seven, and with minor variations in wording, the list pretty much stuck.

> "Disobedience is the true foundation of liberty. The obedient must be slaves."
> —*Henry David Thoreau*

Of course, any classification of human behaviors is arbitrary at best since one man's vice is another man's hobby. Still, the seven "sins" listed below have gotten a consistently bad rap for centuries. But upon closer examination, we can see that context is required in order to properly assess the merits of these spiritual shortcomings:

PRIDE
(a.k.a. vanity) A feeling of superiority based on excessive belief in one's own abilities and importance
WHEN IT'S WRONG: After a successful killing spree
WHEN IT'S RIGHT: When Junior hits his first home run

ENVY
Desire for that which you do not have, or that which your obnoxious neighbor flaunts before you

WHEN IT'S WRONG: If the object of envy is unattainable *(e.g., youth or beauty)*
WHEN IT'S RIGHT: If the object in question is small enough to steal

GLUTTONY

An unusual appetite resulting in the consumption of more that is reasonable or necessary
WHEN IT'S WRONG: In restaurants and social functions
WHEN IT'S RIGHT: At times when no one is looking

LUST

Deep cravings of a polluted mind for physical pleasures and temptations of the flesh
WHEN IT'S WRONG: In the face of probable rejection
WHEN IT'S RIGHT: In the face of probable success

ANGER

(a.k.a. wrath) The rejection of love and the embrace of fury, vengeful feelings and hateful thoughts
WHEN IT'S WRONG: In public settings or on camera
WHEN IT'S RIGHT: When directed at telemarketers or as fuel for fighting injustice

GREED

(a.k.a. avarice) Excessive desire for material wealth, personal gain and a lack of charity toward the less fortunate
WHEN IT'S WRONG: At the corporate level
WHEN IT'S RIGHT: In small, covert endeavors that remain undetected

SLOTH

Laziness and general disinterest in regard to both physical labor and spiritual endeavors

WHEN IT'S WRONG: When the house is on fire

WHEN IT'S RIGHT: On vacation and during the muumuu years *(See Chapter 10)*

THE SEVEN VIRTUES

Of course, there can be no yin without the yang. In the face of vice, there must be virtue, so in contrast to the seven deadly sins, we have a list of seven heavenly principles of morality. But while behaviors such as these may have their merits, they are not necessarily the way to go at all times.

PRUDENCE

Self-discipline and modesty in one's dress, behavior and speech

WHEN IT'S RIGHT: On job interviews

WHEN IT'S WRONG: On dates, at parties or during orgies

TEMPERANCE

Self-restraint, sobriety and frugality in all things, including thoughts and actions

WHEN IT'S RIGHT: In church and when visiting in-laws

WHEN IT'S WRONG: At Christmas parties or whilst writing a book on hedonism

JUSTICE

The fair treatment of others and respect for truth and righteousness

WHEN IT'S RIGHT: In court
WHEN IT'S WRONG: When playing board games

FORTITUDE

The ability to bear misfortune with dignity and to remain courageous in the face of adversity

WHEN IT'S RIGHT: At times of great loss, grief and disappointment

WHEN IT'S WRONG: When being sacked, dumped or cut off

> "When caught between two evils I generally pick the one I've never tried before."
> —*Mae West*

CHARITY

Unselfish generosity, mercy, benevolence and concern for the good of others

WHEN IT'S RIGHT: When cleaning out the closet and donating ugly garments

WHEN IT'S WRONG: Sporting competitions and beauty pageants

HOPE

Idealistic belief and trust in a desired outcome, and the expectation of fulfillment

WHEN IT'S RIGHT: In Las Vegas and at luggage carousels

WHEN IT'S WRONG: When attempting to pay down credit cards

FAITH

Complete trust in one's beliefs and convictions, fidelity and loyalty

WHEN IT'S RIGHT: At the altar
WHEN IT'S WRONG: In the stock market

TEN INSULTING TERMS THAT ARE ACTUALLY
QUITE FLATTERING

One of life's great amusements is when an attempted insult turns out to be a compliment. It's all in the interpretation. So the next time any of these "aspersions" is lobbed in your direction, be sure to smile and say "thank you!"

1. SLUT
WHY? IT MEANS YOU ARE SEXUALLY IRRESISTIBLE.

2. LUSH
WHY? IT'S SHORT FOR LUSCIOUS.

3. MESS
WHY? IT MEANS YOU ARE A CAREFREE BON VIVANT.

4. LIBERAL
WHY? IT MEANS YOU GET INVITED TO THE BEST PARTIES.

5. SELF-INDULGENT
WHY? IT MEANS YOU ARE GOOD TO YOURSELF. THEY HATE THAT.

6. GAUCHE
WHY? IT MEANS YOU HAVE STYLE AND FLAIR.

7. LAZY
WHY? IT MEANS YOU ARE FREE OF STRESS.

8. SHALLOW
WHY? IT MEANS YOU HAVE RETAINED SOME MYSTERY.

9. SUPERFICIAL
WHY? IT MEANS YOU LOOK FABULOUS.

10. HEDONIST
WHY? IT MEANS YOU ARE HAPPY.

MARTYRDOM — JUST DIE ALREADY!

Standing directly to the right of the Pollyanna in the family snapshot of human stereotypes is the martyr. We are not speaking here of the religious zealot who is willing to die for his beliefs, but rather the great and constant sufferer who carries the weight of the world on his or her shoulders—and loves nothing more than whining about it. This is the person who believes that if they don't do it, no one will. They are the only person who cares and who understands the gravity of the situation and must therefore carry the burden.

Such a person must be tormented and ridiculed whenever possible. Martyrdom ranks very high on the list of passive-aggressive behaviors, and it is the duty of any self-respecting hedonist to deflate the balloon of any such silliness wherever it may be found. But to fully enjoy the needling, one must adjust one's tactics according to type.

"Never let your sense of morals keep you from doing what is right."
—*Isaac Asimov*

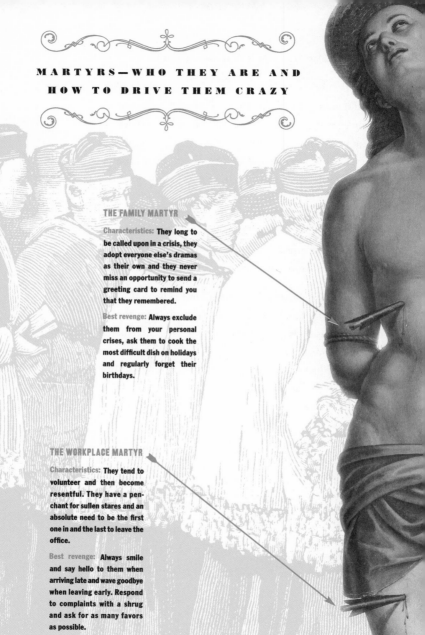

MARTYRS—WHO THEY ARE AND HOW TO DRIVE THEM CRAZY

THE FAMILY MARTYR

Characteristics: **They long to be called upon in a crisis, they adopt everyone else's dramas as their own and they never miss an opportunity to send a greeting card to remind you that they remembered.**

Best revenge: **Always exclude them from your personal crises, ask them to cook the most difficult dish on holidays and regularly forget their birthdays.**

THE WORKPLACE MARTYR

Characteristics: **They tend to volunteer and then become resentful. They have a penchant for sullen stares and an absolute need to be the first one in and the last to leave the office.**

Best revenge: **Always smile and say hello to them when arriving late and wave goodbye when leaving early. Respond to complaints with a shrug and ask for as many favors as possible.**

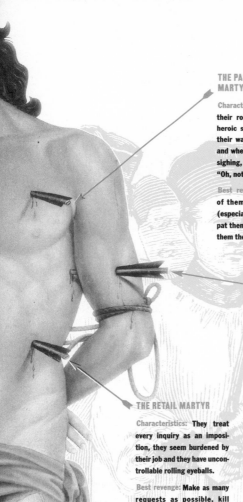

THE PASSIVE-AGGRESSIVE MARTYR

Characteristics: **They accept their role as martyr with a heroic smile, they go out of their way to put others first and when asked why they are sighing, they invariably say, "Oh, nothing."**

Best revenge: **Step in front of them whenever possible (especially in photographs), pat them on the head and tell them they're "cute."**

THE FINANCIAL MARTYR

Characteristics: **They always offer to pay but they examine the bill very seriously for effect, they spend money freely on friends but always keep tabs and they may wait years to reveal their simmering resentment.**

Best revenge: **Offer to pay but immediately give in when they protest, always ask them if they have enough cash on the way out and only give them handmade gifts on birthdays and holidays.**

THE RETAIL MARTYR

Characteristics: **They treat every inquiry as an imposition, they seem burdened by their job and they have uncontrollable rolling eyeballs.**

Best revenge: **Make as many requests as possible, kill them with kindness and talk loudly about your fabulous upcoming vacation on the way out.**

ROMAN WISDOM

In many ways, civilization has evolved tremendously since the days of old, but by the same token, the sheer complexity of life as we know it today can lead us to wonder if we haven't somehow lost the plot. Yes, the Romans could be cruel and vicious—and the body-stink must surely have been horrendous—but at least they were above board about their true nature. They paraded their horrors openly in the coliseums, and backstabbing, adultery and murder were all just part of the game.

"Some cause happiness wherever they go; others whenever they go."
—Oscar Wilde

Today, we believe ourselves to be infinitely superior in terms of ethics, human rights and personal liberties. In some ways we are safer, but in many ways we are not. Few people get fed to the lions these days, but every era produces its own set of horrors. Today we are more closely monitored, more restricted and more heavily policed than ever. This should come as no surprise because the world is now a very dangerous place, but it always has been. And as history steamrolls along, there will always be a mad scramble to gain control of the chaos and to impose upon others the beliefs of those with the strongest will.

The sweeping tides of history may be bigger than any one individual, but at the end of the day, accepting the madness is easier than beating your head against the wall. So think of the Romans. They lived through some crazy shit, but the ones who had a good time and a few laughs amid all the treachery and danger are the ones who are now resting most peacefully.

In Pursuit of Pleasure

IV

"ONLY DULL PEOPLE ARE BRILLIANT
AT BREAKFAST."

— Oscar Wilde

ARE YOU SUFFERING
FROM ANHEDONIA?

HAVE YOU COME TO BELIEVE THAT PLEASURE AND JOY ARE for small children and simpletons? Does the idea of sex seem about as appealing to you as sitting in a puddle? Would you rather eat tin foil than attend a party? If so, you may be suffering from *anhedonia*. Defined as the inability to feel pleasure from what are normally pleasurable experiences, this most treacherous psychological disorder can suck the joy right out of life, leaving the sufferer with a variety of symptoms from indigestion to impotence.

Derived from the Greek, meaning "without pleasure," anhedonia was first identified in the 1890s, but throughout much of the twentieth century it was relegated to the shadows as depression took center stage in the grand theatre of woes and maladies. But unlike depression, it is not characterized by extreme highs and lows, but rather a consistently low mood and the prolonged sense that life is really no more than a flat balloon.

It should come as no surprise that anhedonia is often stress-induced. Even laboratory rats lose interest in the pleasure of the pellet when they are subjected to undue stress, so is it any wonder that a frantic lifestyle and a frenzied pace should jangle the nerves to the point of numbness? The mere existence of such a tragic affliction makes it perfectly clear that leisure and pleasure are essential to ensure stability of mind and sanity in general. If you fear that you are exhibiting even the mildest of anhedonic tendencies, now is the time to take action, to rejoin the living and to step onto the sunny path to recovery.

LEISURE — A BEAUTIFUL WORD

Leisure, according to *The Merriam-Webster Dictionary*, is "freedom provided by the cessation of activities; especially time free from work or duties." It's a simple definition for a simple concept. But in today's hyperkinetic world, leisure is considered by many to be an indulgence or even a decadent extravagance. What was once an integral part of life has been sidelined in favor of hyperproductivity and perpetual motion.

For those racing toward success and the imaginary winner's circle, the mere idea of slowing down and luxuriating in a blissful state of relaxation is terrifying. Thoughts of falling out of the loop, missing important communications or "wasting time" are simply unbearable. Of course, these people are the dream customers of the major pharmaceutical companies that dispense antidepressants and mood elevators like candy to children on Halloween. Each year billions of dollars are made on the misguided premise that happiness and relaxation can be prescribed and purchased in pill form. Get the pills, get happy and keep running.

ARE YOU A HEDONOPHOBE?

Yes there is such a thing. *Hedonophobia* is an intense fear of pleasure that can cause dizziness, shaking, hyperventilation, fear of losing control or a full-blown anxiety attack.

The adverse side effects of an overachieving lifestyle are considerable. In addition to anhedonic depression, high blood pressure, insomnia, irritability, mood swings, ulcers, spastic colons, burnout and heart attacks are but a few of the prizes to be won by those who insist on excessive multitasking and overscheduling. Have we learned nothing from the story of the tortoise and the hare? Who wins in the end? The one who is slow and steady, relaxed and reliable, that's who. The hyperactive bunny crashes on the sidelines and the turtle calmly prevails. And so it goes for the modern hedonist. By living life at a comfortable and leisurely pace, keeping the heart rate down and the mood swings to a minimum, he wins. Not only does he win the game, but he also enjoys the sights along the way. After all, you'll notice a lot more beauty during a leisurely stroll than you will from the window of a bullet train.

A good hedonist knows that leisure is not a luxury or an indulgence, but a true necessity of life, and it is during leisure time that the best things in life take place. Meaningful conversation, thoughtful reflection, spontaneous laughter and human connections rarely occur on a treadmill. Work, exercise and achievement, when practiced in moderation, have their place in the bigger picture, but life is also made up of small moments of joy, periods of unbridled freedom and daily pleasures that must be carefully selected and savored.

BURIED PLEASURES — WHAT USED TO BE FUN

Whatever happened to the three-martini lunch? Or for that matter, whatever happened to lunch? What was once an assumed part of the working day has all but vanished as increasing numbers of Americans find themselves eating lunch out of sad, little Tupperware coffins at their desks, or even worse, in the car. Dinner seems to be hanging on, but for a large number of people lunch has been reduced to little more than a biological pit stop.

It becomes clear that this despicable strangulation of civility is reaching epidemic proportions when workers actually feel guilty about taking the standard hour-long lunch break. This is unacceptable. The time has come for the workers of the world to unite and reclaim this most basic of rights of the workplace. By taking regular, long lunches, citizens will not only restore sanity on the job, they will also contribute to the economy by frequenting restaurants and get valuable exercise on the walk there and back.

In keeping with the theme of midday breaks, the distinguished art of napping has also fallen largely by the wayside. The refreshing pleasures of an afternoon siesta are seen by the zealots of productivity as a sign of lethargy and laziness. However, the seasoned snoozer knows that there is a variety of benefits to be gleaned from a quick nap, on one's own time or at work. Reduced stress,

NAPSTER

Experts say that a nap of 15 to 45 minutes is ideal for a quick afternoon refresher. Anything longer will likely lead to deeper sleep, which can result in grogginess and disorientation.

renewed energy and a general feeling of happiness are all healthy byproducts of the daily nap. These benefits have even been recognized by a handful of progressive corporations that have installed quiet rooms in the workplace where workers can go to drift off and rejuvenate during the workday. It is a highly civilized practice that should rightfully become mandatory, just as handicapped ramps and emergency exits are.

Also ranking high on the list of buried pleasures is sunbathing. Once again, scientific evidence is to blame for sucking the fun out of a good vacation. Ominous reports by sunscreen manufacturers of ozone depletion and increases in skin cancer have yet to clear the lounge chairs of Club Med, but ever-increasing numbers of people are getting their tans out of a tube these days rather than lying beneath the dangerous rays of the demon sun. Spray tanning chambers are the latest technological advance to allow the modern girl- or guy-on-the-go to schedule a bit of color into their agenda. But is it really healthier to stand inside an enclosed chamber inhaling toxic fumes and having your skin artificially stained than to lie in the sun?

The pleasures of tanning are not exclusively rooted in the afterglow. Just as the trees and plants reach toward the sun, humans have a perfectly natural desire to absorb the comforting light and warmth of the golden orb. Sure, most people look better with a little color, and it's always been fun to be practically naked in public, but the most satisfying aspect of tanning lies in the profoundly serene feeling of baking like a lizard on a rock. So with a little SPF in place to counteract the depleting ozone, there's no reason to deny oneself the sensual pleasures of bathing in sunshine.

TEN MOST UNDERRATED PLEASURES

Along with the three-martini lunch, a nice long nap and an afternoon in the sun, there are several other tried-and-true pleasures that must be rescued from the brink of extinction, embraced and revived:

1. FLOATING IN THE OCEAN	6. DIRTY DANCING
✳	✳
2. AFTERNOON COCKTAILS	7. READING IN A HAMMOCK
✳	✳
3. SLEEPING IN	8. CANDLELIT BATHS FOR TWO
✳	✳
4. THE FOOT MASSAGE	9. SITTING IN SILENCE
✳	✳
5. MAKING OUT IN THE RAIN	10. UNCONTROLLABLE LAUGHTER

SIX MEDICAL BENEFITS OF LAUGHTER

The old saying that laughter is the best medicine has turned out to be entirely true. A hearty snort and chuckle can have a variety of healthy side-effects.

1. LAUGHTER BOOSTS THE IMMUNE SYSTEM BY INCREASING THE NUMBER OF CELLS THAT PRODUCE ANTIBODIES.

2. LAUGHTER LOWERS BLOOD PRESSURE. IT INCREASES AT FIRST, BUT

ZZZZZZZZZZZ

According to a 2001 survey, The National Sleep Foundation reports that 63 percent of Americans do not get the recommended eight or more hours of sleep per night during the week.

"The person who knows how to laugh at himself will never cease to be amused."
—*Shirley MacLaine*

THEN STABILIZES AT A LOWER LEVEL.

3. LAUGHTER IS A NATURAL WORKOUT FOR THE DIAPHRAGM AND CAN FACILITATE DIGESTION.

4. LAUGHTER ACTIVATES BOTH SIDES OF THE BRAIN, WHICH INCREASES ALERTNESS AND MEMORY RETENTION.

5. LAUGHTER ELEVATES THE MOOD BY INCREASING CIRCULATION, EASING MUSCLE TENSION AND RELEASING PSYCHOLOGICAL STRESS.

6. LAUGHTER NATURALLY HELPS COMBAT DEPRESSION BY TRIGGERING THE RELEASE OF ENDORPHINS.

MODERN—DAY DECADENCE

For much of recorded history, decadence was defined by thrill-seeking, dangerous behaviors or the pursuit of flat-out oblivion as people sought to arouse their senses to the extreme. A drunken Roman orgy might be capped off with a cleverly plotted murder, church clerics got a quick thrill out of burning witches or torturing heathens, and the occasional tripping hippie might throw up and jump out a window to pull focus at a really groovy party. But those days of splendid excess now seem somewhat passé. The need for extreme stimulation and excitement has waned over time as life itself has become a parade of extremes and more than stimulating enough, thank you.

Ironically, decadence in these days of space-age technology and continuous stimulation is just the opposite of what it once was. That which was crushingly boring in the past, the very thing that drove our forebears to seek excitement and oblivion, is now the ultimate decadent luxury, silence. The intoxicating state we seek is no longer that of the drug-induced stupor, but rather a complete and utter lack of stimulation. Just a few stolen moments away from the television, computer screens, traffic, politics, show business, advertising, neon lights and continuous noise has become either a distant memory or a distant dream of some future escape to a tropical island.

So if you really want to indulge yourself and feel truly decadent, find a quiet spot, read a book, stare at the stars or just sit by the fire and think. Sin may be in, but silence is now in serious vogue.

TEN FUN THINGS YOU NEVER DO ANYMORE

Now that the therapeutic and hedonistic appeal of silence has been established, it should also be pointed out that a life lived without inhibition is equally important. Once the soul has been properly calmed, a little youthful exhilaration can provide just the jolt of stimulation required for a well-balanced life.

1. DANCE LIKE AN IDIOT.	6. DATE NINETEEN-YEAR-OLDS.
2. PLAY ON THE SWINGS.	7. WEAR SEE-THROUGH TOPS.
3. FLASH PEOPLE.	8. MAKE OUT WITH STRANGERS.
4. SWIM DIRECTLY AFTER EATING.	9. GO OUT WITH NO UNDERWEAR.
5. GET HIGH IN YOUR BEDROOM.	10. FLIRT SHAMELESSLY.

LIVING WITHIN YOUR MEANS — POINTLESS

Even the tiresome Dr. Phil acknowledges that "There is no reality; only perception." According to the good doctor, it comes down to understanding the difference between sensation and perception. Clearly, sensations are of great importance to a hedonist, and the good ones are well worth pursuing. As for perception, that has to do with the meaning one ascribes to situations, circumstances and experiences. Life is what you believe it to be based on your interpretation. Tragedy can be perceived as opportunity, loss can be perceived as gain and so on down the line.

This principle is most important to keep in mind when it comes to the subject of money. It isn't real. It was once, when people carried little bags of gold around with them, but now most major financial transactions happen electronically without any cash actually changing hands. Your personal fortune or lack thereof is really no more than an electronic record of numbers held in some distant database. Depending on the prevailing winds, stocks and 401(k)s rise and fall with the global economies, depressions and recessions can make millions of dollars simply evaporate, and nothing is certain except for the guarantee of uncertainty when it comes to the global house of cards we call the economy. And when the inevitable apocalyptic cyberworm wipes everything out, and it will, you'd better have a little bit of gold on hand.

To be sure, debt is a drag, and many of life's pleasures do require money. However, these basic truths need not keep anyone from the good life. This is not to suggest that reckless spending is the path to happiness, but neither is penny pinching. Budgeting spreadsheets and obsessive saving are simply no fun. Having a little nest egg never hurt anyone, but when excessive frugality begins to infringe on your daily enjoyment of life, it's time for a little shopping spree.

The receiving of gifts is usually a pleasurable experience, but rewarding yourself is even better. If you're going to save money, fine, but don't forget to set some aside for a little indulgence. As the old saying goes, you can't take it with you, and if you're "selflessly" stashing it all away to leave to the kids, you are once again drifting toward the dreary abyss of martyrdom.

Of course, extra cash is not always easy to come by, but if in your current circumstance budgeting is required, at least add one line item for a little splurge now and then. It might be as grand as a tropical holiday, or it may just be a new pair of shoes, but regardless of the scale, you owe it to yourself. The world can be a very disappointing place, and other people may let you down, but the one person you can count on to provide that little burst of joy is you. So spend that cash and don't feel guilty. Remember, it is your duty as a good citizen to help maintain the economy. All else is pure selfishness.

HELLO DALAI! — THE MAN WITH THE WORD

"That man is richest whose pleasures are cheapest."
—*Henry David Thoreau*

In the soothingly titled book *The Art of Happiness*, the Dalai Lama offers excellent advice on everything from the true meaning of happiness to the importance of avoiding self-created suffering. The soft-spoken man from Tibet speaks elegantly and eloquently, and with sly and surprising humor. His observations are deliberately simple not because they lack complexity or are anything short of profound, but because many of life's greatest mysteries have very simple answers. And if you're going to take life advice from a stranger, go with the guy who is regularly bedecked in robes the color of sunshine and wine.

According to His Holiness, "If you desire happiness, you should seek the causes that give rise to it, and if you don't desire suffering, then what you should do is to ensure that the causes and conditions that give rise to it no longer arise." Simple, see? And not far from the words of our old friend Epicurus. In other words, life goes by very quickly, and a wise soul does not sleep in itchy pajamas.

TEN PLEASURABLE THINGS TO DO BEFORE YOU DIE

Keeping the bigger picture in mind, the sensible hedonist will not allow him- or herself to be denied the more pleasurable of life's adventures. Though a little juggling, some creative delegation and a balance transfer or two may be required to make them all possible, the following experiences are highly recommended and well worth the effort:

1. GO ON AN ADVENTUROUS VACATION BY YOURSELF. YOU'LL LEARN ABOUT YOURSELF.

＊

2. FALL PASSIONATELY IN LOVE. EMOTIONAL SAFETY ISN'T ALL IT'S CRACKED UP TO BE.

＊

3. VISIT THE TROPICS WITH A LOVER. WHETHER IT LASTS OR NOT, YOU'LL ALWAYS REMEMBER.

＊

4. CAMP OUT IN THE DESERT. ESCAPE FROM CIVILIZATION AND CLARITY WILL COME.

＊

5. RIDE IN A HOT AIR BALLOON. BUT DON'T JUMP UP AND DOWN.

＊

6. SPEND A WEEK AT A RETREAT. ENJOY SHEER INDULGENCE.

＊

7. THROW YOURSELF A SPECTACULAR BIRTHDAY PARTY. IT DOESN'T HAVE TO BE BIG, JUST GRAND.

＊

8. ASSEMBLE A PHOTO ALBUM OF YOUR LIFE. YOU'LL SEE THAT YOUR LIFE HAS A STORY.

＊

9. HAVE A PORTRAIT OF YOURSELF DONE. EVERYONE SHOULD BE IMMORTALIZED FOR POSTERITY.

＊

10. LET GO OF THE PAST. IT'S THERE TO REMEMBER, NOT TO CLING TO.

Clearly, when a top-ten list contains two sentences per entry, there is profundity and philosophy lurking nearby. And though the above-described pursuits of pleasure may seem to be an arbitrary collection of sug-gested indulgences, there is, of course, a larger method and meaning behind the madness. Hedonism is not as shallow as it may seem.

Follow Your Bliss

V

"WE MUST BE WILLING TO GET RID OF THE LIFE WE'VE PLANNED, SO AS TO HAVE THE LIFE THAT IS WAITING FOR US."

— Joseph Campbell

A WORD FROM JOSEPH CAMPBELL

THE SCHOLAR, WRITER AND TEACHER JOSEPH CAMPBELL gained international fame by deconstructing the great mythologies of mankind and revealing the simple truths and profound themes behind history's greatest tales and legends. He drew parallels between classical mythology, modern pop culture and everyday lives. In his view, each life is a hero's journey through which we all are seeking some distant reward, only to discover in the end that we had it in our hands all along. From Odysseus to the Wizard of Oz, it always ends up the same way.

Despite the breadth and scope of his life's work, he is perhaps best known for one simple phrase: "Follow your bliss." The premise is a tantalizingly simple one. If you allow yourself to gravitate toward and pursue that which brings you the greatest pleasure, you will be on the road to achieving personal satisfaction, true happiness and your ultimate calling in life. The idea is to trust your instincts and be aware of when you are happiest and most fully engaged. In doing so, your natural talents will emerge and slowly you will become the person you were intended to be.

In the book *The Power of Myth*, Campbell points out that "If you follow your bliss, you put yourself on a kind of track that has been there all the while, waiting for you, and the life you ought to be living is the one you are living. . . . I say, follow your bliss and don't be afraid, and doors will open for you where you didn't know they were going to be." And if there's one thing a hedonist loves, it's an open door.

Of course, Campbell's epic knowledge of history, art and mythology goes well beyond such basic notions, but time and again in the stories he cites, the elusive, unnamed thing that the hero is seeking is within his grasp all along. Conquering foreign lands, building empires and attempting to rule the world may appeal to the ego, but they do very little for the spirit. And that is precisely why the obscenely rich can never have enough money, the power-crazed must always try to get more and the skinny, skinny TV star who eats but a blade of grass for dinner each night can never be thin enough.

Unfortunately, many of our own personal journeys are thwarted by well-meaning but misguided authority figures who insist that we cannot do in life what we want to do. Life decisions, they tell us, should be made based on economics, practicality or that which may bring us prestige in the eyes of others. We are systematically coaxed onto the treadmill of conventional wisdom and told to start running. These voices that we trust unquestioningly during our impressionable years are often hard to shake, and they silently fuel the manic pace at which we race, all in hopes of receiving some life-affirming pat on the head that may never come.

"People often grudge others what they cannot enjoy themselves."
—Aesop

Happily, it is never too late to get back on the path to personal fulfillment and to a have grand old time doing so. You can live your life on your own terms, or you can wallow forever in the delusion that everyone is judging you and everyone else's opinion counts. In a nutshell, you have a choice. You can allow yourself to be swept up in the daily minutiae, interferences and pettiness of life, or you can move gracefully and quietly along like a panther through the jungle, undistracted and unbothered by the screeching howler monkeys and squawking birds that surround you. Just do your thing, let go of the old voices in your head, accept that which surrounds you and understand that you are not required to react to everything and everyone you encounter.

THE JOY OF GETTING LOST

To the rigidly organized mind, the idea of getting lost is a distinctly unpleasant one and may be fraught with stress. To the happy hedonist, getting lost is an opportunity for adventure and discovery. This is particularly true when shopping, searching for love or when on vacation. To wander freely is to live in a natural state, as God intended. Structure and schedules may serve a purpose in the workplace and at airports, but leisure time is best experienced without an agenda.

You'll never discover that great little restaurant on a side street if you refuse to leave the boulevard, and you may never meet that person who changes your life if you always go to the same places. By leaving a little room in your life for happy accidents and unexpected surprises, you will be continuously maintaining the possibility of magical events occurring. Then again, you may just end up in the shitty end of town, but you can't win every time.

The notion of getting lost does not only apply to direction and destination. It is entirely possible to get completely lost in an activity that is pleasing to you. Just as a child loses all sense of time when playing, a mind that is entirely focused and engaged in the pursuit of delight is freed from the ticking measure of time. This is not a state that can be deliberately achieved, but when it does occur it should be recognized as a sign. When you find yourself in such a state, you know you have found the activity that is right for you. At that point you are deep in pleasure, and that's where you want to be. That is your bliss. And that is what you should be doing more often. Whether it's painting, singing, landscaping or simply spending time with a particular person, recognizing that state of bliss and following it can not only bring you pleasure, it can also help you find your purpose in life, your ideal career or your ideal mate.

If your life has been reduced to a series of tasks, duties and obligations, you have taken a seriously wrong turn at some point and it's time to tap into your inner hedonist. Trust it, listen to it and follow it.

"I haven't failed, I've found 10,000 ways that don't work."
—Thomas A. Edison

THE CREATIVE URGE — ONE PART INSPIRATION, TWO PARTS WINE?

Associations between "creative types" and acts of self-destructive excess are nothing new. The history books are full of alcoholic writers, mad artists, suicidal musicians and drug-addled actors passing through the revolving doors of rehab. So what does that tell us? Do these right-brained artists experience life on a different plane from the buttoned-up business types? Are they really more prone to addiction or merely more flamboyant in the ways they express their inner angst?

The underlying presumption is that by its very nature, the creative urge is unstructured, and those who excel in creative fields tend not to apply structure to their lives as much as, say, the accountant next door. Of course, this theory is flawed in that all arts require some degree of structure, but suspicion and mistrust have always existed between the world's right-brained and left-brained species. In a nutshell, each one thinks the other is nuts.

In the late nineteenth century, a German physician by the name of Max Nordau actually published a book called *Degeneration*, in which he seriously suggested that all the major artists of recent years had proven to be neurotics, alcoholics or drug addicts, or that they were just flat-out insane. He believed that the profusion of art was a sign of social decay and that it actually undermined civilized society. Therefore, he concluded that the healthy mind should at all costs resist the evil influence of art. Quite a hoot, that Max.

Though Herr Nordau's twisted logic may be amusing, there still are plenty of right-wing extremists out there who fly into regular fits of hysteria every time a work of art emerges that upsets their delicate mindset. Such people have yet to fully grasp the "live and let live" philosophy and are not to be invited to the party under any circumstances whatsoever.

> "A life spent making mistakes is not only more honorable, but more useful than a life spent doing nothing."
> —*George Bernard Shaw*

A RETURN TO CHILDHOOD

Much is made of the proverbial return to childhood, but the once-idealized state of childhood is not all that it used to be. For many children, life has become a series of rigidly structured play dates, plastic weight lifting sets and nursery school waiting lists. For the parents of such children, a hard rain is going to fall when those little overachievers grow up and step outside the curriculum. After all, the degree of teenage rebellion directly correlates to the levels of restriction and control imposed during childhood. But looming mutinies aside, there are still a few ways you can recapture those carefree days of utter abandon and hopeless silliness that characterize the ideal state of childhood.

HIJACK YOUR KIDS' TREE HOUSE FOR AN EVENING OF WINE AND CHEESE.

THROW A COCKTAIL PARTY AND REQUIRE GUESTS TO CHOOSE FROM A BASKET OF WIGS.

"IS THERE A DOCTOR IN
THE HOUSE?"

SET UP A TENT IN THE LIVING ROOM AND HAVE A SLUMBER PARTY.

RIDE THE RIDES AT THE STATE FAIR.

GO SLEDDING.

DRAG OUT THE BOARD GAMES.

LEARN TO PLAY A MUSICAL INSTRUMENT.

TAKE AN ART CLASS.

BUILD A SAND CASTLE AT THE BEACH.

PLAY DOCTOR.

A KINKY TALE TO REMEMBER

It is imperative for the modern pleasure seeker to be true to himself throughout his life journey. To live in anticipation of being judged by others or to deny one's true nature can only lead to disappointment and opportunities lost. Following your bliss does not guarantee that you will find the perfect love or make instant connections with others. Life is about trial and error, and it is all part of the eternal quest to find like-minded souls with whom you might share your pleasures. Take in point the case of the kinky guy.

A man is out at a bar and he approaches a woman to whom he feels a strong attraction. They hit it off and he eventually invites her back to his place. On the drive home he tells her, "I think I should tell you up front that I'm a kinky guy. I like kinky things." She smiles at him and purrs reassuringly, "Well, alright."

Upon entering his apartment the woman puts down her purse and removes her coat. The two begin kissing and he whispers in her ear, "I want you to go in the bedroom, take off all your clothes and do a headstand against the wall." Surprised but intrigued, she smiles at him and says, "Alright."

The woman enters the bedroom, undresses, gets herself into a headstand position against the wall and waits. Five minutes pass, then ten, then twenty. Her head full of blood and her temper rising, she climbs down and walks out into the living room, where she finds the man on the couch watching television. "Hello," he smiles.

"What's going on here?" she demands. "I've been in there, naked, standing on my head for twenty minutes! Are you going to do something or not?" He says, "Oh, I did. I shit in your purse."

WHATEVER FLOATS YOUR BOAT

Obviously, there is no accounting for personal taste. Different experiences appeal to different people, but the benevolent hedonist does not judge nor begrudge. As pleasures go, a little experimentation is never a bad thing, but every person has his or her own comfort zone. Misadventures and the occasional unpleasant surprise may be inevitable, but that's no reason to bury your head in the sand and let the parade pass you by. Just trust your instincts, watch your back and be sure to get specifics when a stranger offers a good time.

> "Twenty years from now you will be more disappointed by the things you didn't do than by the ones you did do. So throw off the bowlines. Sail away from the safe harbor. Catch the trade winds in your sails. Explore. Dream. Discover."
> **—Mark Twain**

Indulge Thyself

VI

"BEER IS PROOF THAT GOD LOVES US
AND WANTS US TO BE HAPPY."

- Benjamin Franklin

THE BEAUTY OF THE BUZZ — WISDOM FROM TIMOTHY LEARY AND DEEPAK CHOPRA

ANY DISCUSSION OF HEDONISM MUST ULTIMATELY TOUCH upon the eternal quest for nirvana. Since the beginning of time, human beings have gravitated toward that which feels good, especially that which is forbidden. Intoxication can be alternately liberating, horrifying, blissful, boring, relaxing and frightening. In this regard, it is not unlike marriage or a lengthy dinner party. It all depends on the circumstances, your own mindset and the other people involved.

Intoxication in any form is brought about by a change in brain chemistry. Regardless of whether it is triggered by chocolate, sex, wine, nicotine, morphine or painkillers, the stimulation of neurotransmitters, the release of endorphins or the simple dulling of the senses, intoxication can bring on feelings of ecstasy and escape. And while there are those who quickly condemn any such pursuits as a sign of poor character and weakness, there are others who have a more charitable view of pleasure seeking.

In his book *Overcoming Addiction: The Spiritual Solution*, Deepak Chopra offers the refreshing perspective that addiction is not something that happens to bad people who are in need of punishment. On the contrary, he considers addicts to be "seekers" who are simply searching for a higher ideal, namely enlightenment and inner peace, albeit in all the wrong places. His belief is that the search in itself is a noble one, but the search that leads to chemical addiction is a misguided one. Fair enough. And yes, addiction is a serious matter, not to be taken lightly, and there are alternate means of achieving the aforementioned enlightenment and inner peace, some of which may or may not involve meditation, reflection and challenging, leg-bending poses. But a good hedonist who is lucky enough to avoid addiction is nothing if not creative in his or her rationalizations. Such a person isolates only those parts of any argument that are pleasing to him or her and supports the larger cause. Moving on ...

On the other end of the scale from the Oprah-friendly Chopra, we find the radical '60s guru of the counterrevolution. It was Dr. Timothy Leary, a psychology professor at Harvard in the 1950s, who coined the '60s mantra "turn on, tune in, drop out." Leary and many other psychologists of the day believed that LSD (or acid, as the kids called it) had therapeutic and spiritual benefits, and that when administered in controlled doses, it could be used for everything from reforming criminals to treating alcoholism. His experiments involving graduate students, along with his generally radical ideas, eventually got him tossed out of Harvard, but throughout his colorful life of FBI raids, prison sentences and life abroad, he always maintained that humans had eight "circuits of consciousness," but that most only ever accessed four of them. Like Chopra, he believed that the

THE GREEN FAIRY

Absinthe, or the Green Fairy as it was once quaintly known, is an extremely potent herbal liqueur containing a variety of herbs, including anise, licorice, fennel, lemon balm and, most notably, wormwood. Though it usually contains roughly sixty percent alcohol, it is supposedly the wormwood that triggers the buzz of legend. The emerald green liqueur, usually served with ice water and a cube of sugar, was wildly popular among Parisian bohemians in the 1840s, and later among artists and writers including Vincent Van Gogh, Oscar Wilde and Ernest Hemingway. By 1915 it was considered to be an opiate and was banned in most countries, but legal brands are still available in several European countries, and its popularity is once again increasing, proving that the wildly intoxicating allure of the Green Fairy lives on.

deeper levels of consciousness could be accessed through meditation and spirituality, but he is best remembered for his suggested shortcuts.

The parallel to be drawn here is that these two very public voices, from opposite extremes, agree on one larger theme—that the opening of the mind and the pursuit of enlightenment are tricky businesses at best. But left to our own devices, without access to chemistry labs or monasteries but with a sense of personal responsibility, we are all ultimately responsible for our own journeys. Caution is key and the perils are many, but so it is with life in general.

DRINKING

Alcohol should always be kept away from children, as they are entirely reckless and sloppy enough in their natural states. However, the laughable attempts of the past to prohibit alcohol consumption have proven that as far as adults are concerned, the genie is out of the bottle and there's no turning back. Though there are still some countries where it is legally banned, in most cultures of the world alcohol has become an integral part of the very fabric of society. It is used to toast successes, to cushion the blow of personal failures, to mourn losses and to celebrate holidays. After all, what fun is an Irish wake without the booze? Who eats sushi without sake? And what's a wedding without a bridesmaid throwing up in the bushes?

Alcohol has always played an important role as a social lubricator of sorts in that it lowers inhibitions, thereby allowing us to reveal more of ourselves than we might ordinarily be willing to show. Of course, we are speaking here of baring the soul, not the breasts at a Christmas party, but that's always good for a laugh too. But on a much higher plane, cocktails can add a magical touch to an average experience, a romantic interlude or a painfully dull evening. That said, they can also lead to an unplanned new baby or to the downward slide of a self-destructive soul. But as always, excess must be carefully measured, and a crippling hangover is nature's punishment for poor judgment. Hence, we can see once again that biology is our guide.

TEN BENEFITS OF THE POST-WORK HAPPY HOUR

1. DISCOUNT COCKTAILS

2. THE OPPORTUNITY FOR VENTING

3. A SAFE ARENA FOR OFFICE GOSSIP

4. A NATURAL WEEDING OUT OF THE NERDS

5. BONDING WITH FELLOW ALCOHOLICS

6. DATING BARTENDERS

7. DECREASE OF STRESS LEVELS

8. AN EXCUSE TO AVOID THE GYM

9. POTENTIAL SEX WITH HOT COWORKERS

10. VALUABLE BLACKMAIL MATERIAL ON THE BOSS

THE TEN MOST LUSH-OUS STATES

In the year 2000, the Alcohol Epidemiologic Data Directory indicated that 64 percent of the U.S. population drank alcohol, and that the average American consumed 2.18 gallons of ethyl alcohol annually. The state-by-state statistics seem to indicate that snow, gambling and the rigors of a life in politics all play a significant role in the thirst for oblivion. Behold the top ten states in annual, per capita alcohol consumption:

NEW HAMPSHIRE	4.00 GALLONS
NEVADA	3.67 GALLONS
WASHINGTON, D.C.	3.53 GALLONS
DELAWARE	2.89 GALLONS
WISCONSIN	2.76 GALLONS
ALASKA	2.63 GALLONS
COLORADO	2.60 GALLONS
FLORIDA	2.55 GALLONS
MASSACHUSETTS	2.53 GALLONS
MONTANA	2.55 GALLONS

"Nothing more excellent or valuable than wine was ever granted by the Gods to man."
–Plato

(Utah ranked lowest with 1.27 gallons per person. Surprise!)

DRUGS

A *drug*, by definition, is any chemical introduced to the body that alters the mental state or bodily functions. Therefore, there is no one on the planet in this twenty-first century who can accurately claim, "I don't take drugs." From aspirin to acid, vitamins to Vicodin, we are all guilty of toying with our natural chemistry on a daily basis. But when it comes to the plethora of drugs available to the modern consumer, be they natural or man-made, the tangle of legalities and official classifications are both mind-boggling and, at times, seemingly arbitrary.

"Water? Never touch the stuff! Fish fuck in it."
—*W. C. Fields*

Any adult is free to purchase beer, coffee and cigarettes at the corner deli, but a small bag of marijuana can only be purchased through an illegal transaction. The variety of stimulants, barbiturates and narcotics that can be prescribed by doctor is staggering, while others can only be purchased illicitly at your local rave or through clandestine personal connections. Over the years, laws have been passed, revoked, reinstated and rethought countless times in a never-ending quest to monitor the endless array of chemicals with which the masses toy. But if time has taught us anything, it is that people will always find a way to get their buzz on.

The ongoing arguments about the legalization of certain drugs are often disguised as moral debates or noble battles to protect the public's health. But in fact, at the very root of all the rhetoric, it all comes down to cash. The simple truth is that there is money to be made in the drug trade, and the question is always a matter of who will profit in the end. Today, international pharmaceutical companies are earning inconceivable amounts of money each year by catering to the neuroses and insecurities of the public at large. Not only is their business legal, it is freely promoted through television advertising. You can't advertise cigarettes or hard liquor on television, but erection pills and mood elevators are more than welcome on the airwaves.

In actuality, much of the advertising can be quite entertaining. Somber voices in television commercials ask probing questions such as "Do you ever feel listless, tired or uninterested? Would you like to be more outgoing at parties? Do your thoughts sometimes wander?" If you have fallen victim to any of these terrifying symptoms, you are apparently in some deep shit and need medical attention pronto. Luckily there are a variety of 'zins, 'zacs, 'olofts and 'osets to help you find your way back to the ordinary world, so whip out the checkbook, Nancy! The reassuring TV voice usually trails off slightly at the end of such commercials, warning that side effects may include diarrhea, constipation, dizziness, nausea, migraines, difficulty urinating or searing stomach pains, but these are minor issues when one has the opportunity to purchase happiness in pill form. One particularly amusing commercial promoting a cure for erectile dysfunction casually comes to a close with the sensible warning that "erections lasting more than four hours may require medical attention." Really? Apparently, a three-and-a-half hour stiffy is not a problem.

As the public is slowly hypnotized into believing that

their human emotions require expensive medication, the prison system is simultaneously becoming overpopulated and overburdened by hundreds of thousands of "drug offenders" whose true crime may just be that they didn't buy the *approved* drugs. So a high-rolling corporate executive may be free to float through life on the mind-numbing wings of prescribed narcotic painkillers, but if Grandma smokes a joint in her little apartment to ease the effects of glaucoma and lessen the discomforts of cancer, she'll be hauled off to prison with murderers, terrorists and rapists where she belongs. Ironic.

As for addiction, anyone and everyone is susceptible, but not all drugs are physically addictive, and limited use of addictive drugs does not necessarily lead to addiction. There are a variety of factors that contribute to addiction, and people who are mentally healthy, have stable jobs, relationships and support systems, and have no familial history of addiction may be less vulnerable to addiction. Of course, you never know, but it is naïve to assume that legal drugs are less dangerous than illegal ones when it comes to addiction. Nicotine is more addictive than heroin, and while marijuana is considered nonaddictive, pain killers are notoriously addictive.

In the end, as always, it all comes down to personal responsibility and accountability. A sensible hedonist is not a reckless risk-taker. As Epicurus always said, pleasure that leads to pain is to be avoided. But at the same time, a true hedonist is a purist and does not appreciate being manipulated by global conglomerates and political agendas. Measured pleasure is the name of the game, and personal choice goes hand in hand with self-protection.

WHAT THEY ARE, WHAT THEY DO AND WHO LOVES THEM

MARIJUANA

WHAT IT IS: Pot, hash

WHAT IT DOES: The smoking of either substance usually results in feelings of relaxation, mood elevation and general sedation, though the effects of hash are usually somewhat more intense. Emotional reactions range widely from person to person and may include fits of laughter, moments of profound contemplation, feelings of paranoia or the sudden realization that the world is really a fucked-up place.

WHO LOVES IT: Old hippies, creative types and college students

WHAT THE RISKS ARE: Lethal overdose is virtually unknown when it comes to marijuana. At worst, a user may experience feelings of anxiety or may become psychologically dependent. Getting high does effect motor abilities and can cause focus to drift, so driving under the influence is not advised. Pot smokers often draw attention to themselves when driving by having the

ANCIENT CHINESE SECRET

Enkephalins and endorphins are natural opiates produced by the brain, and studies have shown that the production of such opiates can be triggered and even increased through acupuncture. The natural chemicals in turn produce feelings of pleasure, stress reduction and the suppression of physical pain.

windshield wipers on when it's not raining or driving with the windows rolled down during snowstorms.

SEDATIVES

WHAT THEY ARE: Alcohol, barbiturates, Quaaludes, GHB, Valium, Xanax, etc.

WHAT THEY DO: Sedatives increase relaxation and reduce anxiety, but in higher doses can result in drowsiness, slurred speech, impaired motor abilities and humiliating photographs.

WHO LOVES THEM: Just about everyone

WHAT THE RISKS ARE: Though benzodiazepines (mild relaxants like Valium, Xanax, etc.) alone rarely result in fatal overdoses, all other sedatives taken in excessive quantities can lead to death by heart failure or suppression of breathing, and all sedatives are dangerous when mixed with other sleep-inducing drugs.

OPIATES

WHAT THEY ARE: Opium, heroin, morphine, Percodan, Demerol, Vicodin, etc.

WHAT THEY DO: Opiates produce a rush of pleasure followed by a dreamy state of relaxation. They also decrease sensitivity to pain and usually lead to droopy eyelids, dopey grins and occasional spooky thoughts.

MONKEY BUSINESS

In the late 1950s, legendary screen idol Cary Grant embarked on a long program of LSD therapy administered in controlled situations by psychiatrists who believed in the therapeutic benefits of the drug. In subsequent years, Grant freely praised the experiences claiming that they had freed him of psychological trauma he had been suppressing for decades. In the biography *CG: A Touch of Elegance*, he suavely surmises, "You know we are all unconsciously holding our anus."

WHO LOVES THEM: Tortured souls, thrill-seekers and dental patients

WHAT THE RISKS ARE: Opiates can be lethal even on a first-time basis if taken in sufficient doses. The strong effect of relaxation can easily lead to the complete cessation of breathing.

STIMULANTS

WHAT THEY ARE: Cocaine, crack, speed, amphetamines, Ritalin, etc.

WHAT THEY DO: Stimulants increase energy, provide feelings of alertness and heightened awareness, and stimulate pointless conversation.

WHO LOVES THEM: Type A personalities, overachievers, underachievers and terrified celebrities

WHAT THE RISKS ARE: Even a single use of stimulants can result in seizures, cardiac arrest, breathing cessation or stroke if taken in a high enough dosage. Also, long-term use can have psychiatric effects, such as increasing paranoia or hostility.

ENTACTOGENS

WHAT THEY ARE: Ecstasy, MDMA and its variations

WHAT THEY DO: MDMA (methylenedioxymethamphetamine) increases the heart rate, body temperature and blood pressure. It also produces feelings of euphoria, energy and physical pleasure, which in turn often lead to lots of touching, ill-advised sexual trysts and stupid confessions.

WHO LOVES THEM: Ravers, sex addicts and men in midlife crisis

WHAT THE RISKS ARE: When combined with physical exertion, the drug can bring on heightened body temperature, hypertension, kidney failure or even death.

HALLUCINOGENS

WHAT THEY ARE: Acid, magic mushrooms, mescaline, PCP, etc.

WHAT THEY DO: Hallucinogens can alter one's sense of time and space, producing visual and sensory experiences that are not reality-based. They can also contribute to a sense of separation of body and mind, leading to altered perceptions, feelings of spiritual or intellectual insight, and embarrassingly large pupils.

WHO LOVES THEM: Artists, scientists and free-thinkers

WHAT THE RISKS ARE: Use of hallucinogens such as LSD and magic mushrooms may result in a "bad trip," causing the user to experience extreme anxiety, paranoia or self-injury if judgment is severely impaired. PCP and other such compounds are far more dangerous and can result in coma, cardiac arrest or even death.

INHALANTS

"You never know what is enough unless you know what is more than enough."
—*William Blake*

WHAT THEY ARE: Anesthetics, poppers, nitrous oxide, whippets, paints, glues, fuels, etc.

WHAT THEY DO: Anesthetics administered by a trained physician initially cause feelings of dreamlike relaxation, ultimately giving way to major sedation. Chemical inhalants used for "recreational" purposes cause blood pressure to drop while simultaneously causing the heart rate to rise. Mild euphoria and the lowering of inhibitions are short-lived and are often followed by a great big headache.

WHO LOVES THEM: Surgical patients, bored teenagers and morons

WHAT THE RISKS ARE: While inhaled nitrites rarely result in lethal overdose, they do suppress breathing and lower heart rates, and they can be very dangerous. The inhalation of solvents is extremely dangerous and can result in loss of consciousness, heart attack and death, even from a single experience. Even anesthetics can be fatal if dosages are not properly monitored, so never be rude to your anesthesiologist.

EVERYTHING IS JUUUST FIIINE

While Utah may have the lowest rate of annual alcohol consumption in the nation, according to a 2002 article in the *Los Angeles Times*, it also has the highest rate of prescriptions written for antidepressants. The same article also reported that Utah ranked first among the states in the use of narcotic painkillers.

ADDICTION

Addiction is clearly a serious matter, and countless studies have been performed to determine which drugs are addictive and which drugs aren't. It is fairly common knowledge that stimulants such as cocaine or speed, opiates such as heroin, and alcohol, nicotine and some painkillers are the most addictive drugs. Marijuana and LSD are generally not thought to be addictive, though a user may become psychologically dependent. But habitual use is not the same thing as addiction, which seems to take hold in the neural circuitry of the brain.

"I've said I've never broken the drug laws of my country, and that is the absolute truth."
—*Bill Clinton*

In both humans and animals, the brain is hard-wired to experience pleasure from activities that sustain the species. That's why sex feels good, water quenches thirst and food alleviates hunger. It's Mother Nature's way of ensuring that we repeat these essential behaviors and keep the biological party in full swing. It is the stimulation of certain neural circuits and the release of dopamine that reinforces the behaviors, and this in turn sets in motion a pattern of repetition.

Tests have shown that nicotine, alcohol, stimulants and opiates stimulate this same circuit of dopamine production. Addiction can be extremely powerful because it can take hold at a very deep and primal level, at a level on par with the instinct for survival. And that is why a coked-up rat in a cage will forsake food, sex and anything else to press on a bar to the point of exhaustion just to get another fix. The rat truly comes to believe he can't survive without it. And it can get just as ugly for a human. When the avoidance of the pain and discomfort of withdrawal begins to feel like a fight to survive and when the desire to use feels close to a thirst, a hunger or an overwhelming drive, you are in way too deep and need to make that phone call.

And now, on to a far more pleasing subject . . .

SEX

In the realm of earthly pleasures, none has the capacity to thrill, excite and fascinate more than the age-old favorite of sex. In the beginning, sex was just sex. It was a deeply rooted, primitive urge that served the sole biological purpose of perpetuating the species. And biology dictated that in order for any species to want to regularly engage in what is really a rather exhausting endeavor, it had to feel really good. It did then and it still does. But the relationship between sex and love has changed considerably throughout history.

As civilizations evolved around the globe, communities were established and the notion of the family unit began to take hold. In time the concept of marriage was born. But marriage in the old days was little more than a business arrangement between families, and in many parts of the world it still is. During the height of the Roman Empire, a marriage was simply a household arrangement, and sex was a vigorous, lusty, guilt-free form of recreation to be enjoyed at every opportunity. Prostitutes

"Every form of addiction is bad, no matter whether the narcotic be alcohol or morphine or idealism."
—**Carl Gustav Jung**

and courtesans were held in relatively high esteem, and the mere idea of a monogamous marriage would seem preposterous to the average citizen, who would surely see no reason to bypass a perfectly good orgy.

It wasn't until Christianity took hold and Rome began its historic decline that sex began to be associated with guilt, sin and shame. Christians associated the Roman downfall with sex and pleasure, and over time the tedious practices of self-denial, abstinence and self-torture took their place. Sin was out and guilt was in. Humanity began a headlong plunge into the dark ages, and by the fifth century the institution of marriage fell under the control of the all-powerful clergy. Sex became a dirty, shameful act that was only to be engaged in when absolutely necessary. Of course, none of this prevented members of the clergy or the powerful elite from taking mistresses or sexually abusing others, but they hated themselves for it and that's what really counted.

By the eleventh century, a romantic ideal began to take form and the age of poetry and courtship began. Abstinence was still the respectable route to salvation, but courtly love swept across Europe in a big way and emotion had wormed its way into the boudoir. By the time the Renaissance was in full swing in the 1400s, the dark forces of organized religion were in a pitched battle with the new spirit of the day and with the sinful notions of rationalism and personal happiness. As a

"In America sex is an obsession, in other parts of the world it is a fact."
—*Marlene Dietrich*

MY, WHAT A GLAMOROUS DILDO YOU HAVE!

Dildos were always very popular among ladies in ancient Greece and Rome. Though crude models were crafted from animal horns, the more elegant models were made of gold, silver, ivory or glass.

result, lots of hilarity ensued with seductive women being burned as witches, crazed fanatics flagellating themselves and religious dissenters falling prey to a whimsical Inquisition complete with mass murder, widespread torture and general intolerance taken to psychotic extremes. Still, the Age of Enlightenment had arrived, science was being used to debunk centuries of superstition and fear, and the middle classes were beginning to wonder if love and sex were really all that bad.

By the time the Puritans came along, sex within the confines of marriage was seen as a good and wholesome thing, but adulterers and other deviants risked whippings, public humiliation or even execution. By the mid-eighteenth century, unbridled emotion began to fall out of fashion in favor of intellectualism and reason. Formal manners and strict codes of etiquette were the order of the day, and self-control was the ideal *du jour*. The standards of high morality only escalated during the Victorian era, especially for women, but modern influences such as international travel, popular pornography and opium helped to spice things up a bit. By the time of the Industrial Revolution, the middle class was growing and personal freedom could once again be glimpsed looming on the horizon.

With the advent of the twentieth century came the empowerment of women and the revolution of birth control. Women were finally able to enjoy sex freely, as men had for so many centuries, without the nagging prospect of ending up with a screaming gaggle of children. But all the while, as the church began to lose its hold on popular morality, the government was waiting in the wings with armloads of documentation to help regulate the pleasures of the masses. After all, someone had to control the maniacs.

"That which we call sin in
others is experiment for us."
—*Ralph Waldo Emerson*

So today we are freer, but not entirely free. Legislative battles over personal freedoms still drag on, and probably always will. But such is progress. It takes time. But through it all, the wise hedonist proceeds calmly amidst the hysteria, knowing that there will always be repressed individuals out there who cannot abide the idea that others are out there having the fun that they so rigorously deny themselves. Tortured as they are, these perturbed souls preach and judge and condemn. And they should be allowed to do so, not because they deserve to be heard, but because it keeps them out of life's grand, collective bedroom while the rest of us enjoy ourselves.

APHRODISIACS

From rhinoceros horns to sparrow brains, various substances, potions and foods have been thought to stimulate the libido and increase sexual desire. While many of the legendary theories were based on guesswork and superstition, there are some that seem to have some scientific merit behind their reputation as lust elixirs.

OYSTERS: Commonly believed to be an aphrodisiac, the obscenely slippery oyster is actually rich in zinc, which is an essential mineral that can increase production of testosterone.

ASPARAGUS: Phallic shape aside, asparagus contains high levels of potassium, phosphorus, calcium and vitamin E, all of which can contribute to sex hormone production.

CHILI PEPPERS: Not only do they chemically stimulate nerve endings, induce sweating and raise the pulse, they can also stimulate the release of endorphins to bring on the mood.

CHOCOLATE: If only by releasing those love endorphins, chocolate can arouse amorous feelings. External application in syrup form can also help establish a mood.

YOHIMBE: Yohimbe bark contains an amino acid called arginine that can stimulate the nervous system and increase blood flow to the genitals. However, anxiety, nausea and raised blood pressure can put a bit of a damper on the proceedings.

GINGKO: Though often taken for memory loss, gingko can also help with erection loss. The release of nitric oxide widens blood vessels and increases blood flow.

DAMIANA: A wild yam, damiana is said to contain natural chemicals that can increase genital sensitivity and even induce erotic dreams.

SPANISH FLY: The illegal aphrodisiac of lore is actually made from the dried husk of a beetle. Its alarming effect is to produce irritation in the genital membranes, but it is also very dangerous and can result in kidney malfunction, intestinal hemorrhaging and even death. Not so sexy, after all.

TOP FIVE HEALTH BENEFITS OF REGULAR SEX

The peculiar attempts of both church and state to regulate sexual activity are not only immoral, they are counterproductive to the health and happiness of the population at large. When practiced with sensible precautions and social responsibility, good sex contributes to the sanity, stability and serenity of society by contributing to the general well-being of the individual. Behold the benefits:

1. REDUCED RISK OF HEART DISEASE
VIGOROUS CARDIOVASCULAR ACTIVITY CAN SIGNIFICANTLY REDUCE THE RISK OF HEART ATTACK AND STROKE.

2. WEIGHT LOSS / IMPROVED FITNESS
AN ENTHUSIASTIC ROMP IN THE SACK CAN BURN UP TO 200 CALORIES AND WORK OUT A VARIETY OF MUSCLES.

3. DEPRESSION AND STRESS REDUCTION
THE PHYSICAL RELEASE OF ORGASM CAN RESULT IN PROFOUND RELAX-ATION, BETTER SLEEP AND IMPROVED CIRCULATION.

4. FEWER COLDS AND FLUS
REGULAR SEX INCREASES PRODUCTION OF IMMUNOGLOBULIN A, AN ANTIBODY THAT BOOSTS THE IMMUNE SYSTEM.

5. PAIN RELIEF
INCREASED LEVELS OF THE HORMONE OXYTOCIN IN TURN RELEASE ENDORPHINS THAT CAN ALLEVIATE A MULTITUDE OF PHYSICAL PAINS, FROM HEADACHES TO JOINT PAIN.

FIVE CUTE TERMS FOR POST-9/11 SEX

In the age of terrorism and SARS, a sense of urgency has found its way into the minds of many. Long-term visions of romantic bliss have given way to one-night stands and immediate gratification. For better or worse, the common vernacular always reflects the trends that bind. Here are five new terms for the modern quickie:

☞ Armageddon sex
☞ Apocalypse sex
☞ Terror sex
☞ Anxiety fling
☞ Disaster tryst

FOOD

In the current climate of carbohydrate demonization, calorie counting and food fascism, it is estimated that one in every five Americans is vigorously adhering to a fad diet of some sort. As the never-ending quest for physical perfection reduces healthy humans to insecure, self-loathing wretches, pharmaceutical companies and annoyingly perky personal trainers are profiting wildly on the insecurities that are in turn perpetuated by unrealistic ideals. Sure, it's great to be thin. You can wear better clothes and you get more attention. But a thin person with no confidence has nothing on her zaftig counterpart who radiates health and sexual confidence. To be clear, the skinny may get some of the spoils in today's society, but sexual attraction is a mysterious thing, so if you think you can't eat and still get laid, you are a fool.

In the face of the current epidemic of structured self-denial, there is a bright light in the world of pop-culture cooking. She is Nigella Lawson, the buxom and sultry Brit who purrs across the television airwaves that her one rule of the kitchen is "If it tastes good, eat it." Her unabashed embrace of kitchen hedonism is a strong call for the very best kind of indulgence and is the perfect excuse for her incessant, heavy-lidded finger licking, which has elevated her from the realms of the average to an iconic sex bomb with a spatula. Add to the equation the fact that her television program is called *Nigella Bites*, and it becomes undeniably clear that she has a deep and profound understanding of the appeal of naughty pleasures.

Seemingly healthy in every way, this wife, mother and entrepreneur whips up recipes from scratch, using real ingredients in generous amounts. And though she may not be stick-thin, the voluptuous and contented persona she projects is the perfect advertisement for good living of the most satisfactory type. Self-deprivation, second-rate substitutes and corner-cutting have no place in Nigella's world, nor should they in yours. Healthy eating is not just about skinless chicken breasts, whipped egg whites or salad dressings ordered on the side. It is about well-prepared food, made from natural ingredients served in reasonably-sized portions.

Grazing on bottomless bags or boxes of processed foods is neither satisfying nor pleasurable so much as it is distracting and deceptive. Munching continuously on an endless supply of chips offers no variety, no sensuality and no true stimulation of the palate. The true measure of pleasure in a meal is found in its combination of flavors, textures and even colors. Nature offers a spectacular variety of sensations and subtleties to experience and savor, and a true hedonist knows that in order to be fully enjoyed, dining must be an active, conscious experience, not an exercise in shoveling and gobbling. Nigella would tell you the same.

COCOA LOVE

Phenylethylamine is a natural chemical, similar to an amphetamine, found in chocolate. By releasing endorphins, it produces some of the same euphoric effects brought on by sexual attraction and love.

"Be careful about reading health books. You may die of a misprint."
—*Mark Twain*

TEN MOST SATISFYING HIGH-CARB FOODS

Hey, we don't all have Oprah Winfrey's metabolism, so there's no reason not to enjoy some of the most satisfying foods available. On occasion, in limited amounts, these culinary delights will give you the extra boost of energy you'll need for a quick swim directly after eating:

1. BAGUETTES	6. BAGELS
✳	✳
2. FRENCH FRIES	7. BREAKFAST CEREALS
✳	✳
3. PASTA	8. DONUTS
✳	✳
4. PASTRIES	9. COOKIES
✳	✳
5. FRIED RICE	10. BEER

THE DISEASE OF THE RICH

Gout, a disease often ascribed to "rich living," is actually a form of arthritis that usually affects the joints of the feet and ankles, and most commonly the joint of the big toe. Contributing factors to the development of gout include a high alcohol intake, obesity, and excessive amounts of rich foods such as red meat, shellfish and cream sauces.

THE FRENCH PARADOX

Studies have shown that the French eat 30 percent more fat than their American counterparts, yet they suffer 40 percent fewer heart attacks. Not only that, but the majority of them are annoyingly thin as well, though that may have more to do with their incessant smoking rather than diet. But body issues aside, more than a hundred scientific studies have shown that moderate consumption of red wine can have positive effects on one's health, assisting in the prevention of heart disease, high blood pressure and even certain cancers. It seems that regular consumption of red wine helps to raise the levels of "good" cholesterol while lowering levels of "bad" cholesterol, and can therefore actually help prevent heart attacks and strokes. Even the World Health Organization reports that moderate consumption of red wine (no more than 2–3 units per day for women, 3–4 units for men) can have a protective effect against coronary heart disease. And, far more importantly, it also improves the dinner conversation.

FORGET YOUR SNIFFLES, C'MON GET HAPPY

Multiple studies have shown that in addition to helping prevent heart disease, regular consumption of red wine can also help reduce the risk of contracting the common cold by as much as 44 percent.

This is a prime example of the futility of trying to outsmart Mother Nature and the natural inclinations she has endowed us with. After thousands of years, science has finally proven that there is good to be found in the very human attraction to that which feels and tastes good. In fact, the largest such study—the Copenhagen City Heart Study—actually stated that "Consumption of 1 or 2 drinks per day is associated with a reduction in risk of dying from coronary heart disease of approximately 30–50 percent." It went on to state, "Because coronary heart disease accounts for one third or more of total death, people with no alcohol consumption have higher total mortality than those drinking 1 to 2 drinks per day."

Of course, alcoholics may need to turn to green tea or pharmaceuticals to extend their life spans, and there is hope on the horizon for those who are unable to imbibe. Scientists in Italy are said to be developing a pill that will simulate all the beneficial effects of wine consumption. But for those who are avoiding alcohol in a misguided effort to improve their health, a little reevaluation may be in order. If you can, you should. It's fun and it's civilized, so pop the cork and get with the program!

SMOKING

Evidence suggests that the tobacco plant began growing in the Americas as long ago as 6000 B.C. And history tells us that by 3000 B.C., on the other side of the world, the Egyptians had ritualized the seductive allure of smoke through the burning of herbs and incense in sacrificial ceremonies. But the earliest indications of the actual practice of tobacco smoking can be traced back to the Maya and Aztec civilizations in roughly the first century B.C., when tobacco was rolled in leaves or stuffed inside unwieldy bamboo shoots for what was surely a rather harsh experience.

Christopher Columbus was the first European to document the strange and exotic practice as he sailed throughout the Caribbean Seas in 1492. Sensing an opportunity for profit, the Europeans soon began to cultivate the new crop, and by the mid-sixteenth century pipe-smoking had become a radical and exotic practice of which the Europeans became very suspicious. But within the next one hundred years the groovy new fad took hold, and pipe, cigar and, ultimately, cigarette smoking became fairly commonplace. By the mid–1800s, commercially manufactured cigarettes were being produced, and tobacco's slow seduction of the planet was underway.

By the turn of the twentieth century, smoking had taken on a sexually seductive subtext. Decadent plumes of smoke rising from the elegant fingertips of an exotic beauty suggested mystery and drama. A man lighting a cigarette with his eyes fixed on someone across a crowded room held untold promises, and the lazy, jaded mood of cabaret theater only became more exotic when viewed through a floating haze of smoke. Cigarettes filled silences, and more importantly, as sexual liberation was coming back into vogue, they provided a new and socially acceptable way for the sexes to approach one another. "Have you got a light?"

BOTTOMS UP

It is believed that Peruvian Aguaruna aboriginals used tobacco not only for chewing and smoking, but also for exhilarating hallucinogenic enemas.

In the cinema, smoking was glamorized as never before with stars like Marlene Dietrich, Humphrey Bogart, Bette Davis and Cary Grant raising smoking to an art form. A long drag of the cigarette could suspend a dramatic moment, it could be used as a wand of seduction, and it provided exquisite punctuation if a shattering line of dialogue was immediately followed by the snuffing out of the cigarette. Smoking had become a sign of sophistication and cigarette consumption escalated dramatically.

Though the statistical correlation between smoking and cancer was discovered by German scientists as early as the 1930s, the public remained blissfully unaware as they puffed and posed their way through the next several decades. By 1939, it was reported that more than 50 percent of the American male population smoked. In

1952, the filtered cigarette was introduced as the public began to get wind of the ominous scientific studies, though cigarette companies publicly refuted the evidence of harmful side effects. The supreme irony that cigarette manufacturers advertised their new filtered cigarettes as a "healthy" alternative was only heightened by the fact that the original filters were made of asbestos. But through it all, the public continued its love affair with cigarettes. People from all walks of life enjoyed the decadent delight, not because they were self-destructive, but because it felt good.

It wasn't until 1964 that the first Surgeon General's report definitively stating the health hazards of smoking was released. Eventually the scientific evidence became irrefutable, and smoking began to decline, at least in Western Europe and North America. But interestingly, statistics show that after every major war in recent history, smoking has increased. Of course, that may be largely due to the fact that soldiers, from the Civil War through World War II, were given rations of cigarettes by the government. Even so, it is during times of great stress that ex-smokers often cave, and in the post-9/11 climate, as smokers defiantly huddle on the streets of London, New York and LA, puffing away madly, it would seem that this theory holds true.

Today the glamour and pleasure of smoking have been significantly dampened, and for those who haven't already been seduced, it is obviously unwise to begin.

But for those who do smoke, the issue is largely one of personal freedom. Addiction is clearly part of the picture, but how an individual chooses to deal with his own addiction cannot be legislated. If secondhand smoke is indeed a danger, smokers will move to the sidewalk. If cigarettes are taxed, they will find the extra money. And if smoking is stigmatized, they will defiantly hold their ground. When behaviors are banned, they often turn into fetishes. And human beings love their fetishes, despite the hazards.

TEN REASONS SMOKERS KEEP SMOKING

1. INSTANT BONDING WITH OTHER SMOKERS

*

2. AN EXCUSE TO LEAVE THE OFFICE

*

3. THE CALMING EFFECTS OF DEEP BREATHING—JUST LIKE YOGA!

*

4. THE STUBBORN REJECTION OF AUTHORITY

*

5. SATISFACTION OF AN ORAL FIXATION

*

6. WEIGHT CONTROL

*

7. COMPLETE LACK OF SELF-CONTROL

*

8. BAD BOY / BAD GIRL COMPLEX

*

9. QUITTING IS A DRAG

*

10. IT FEELS GOOD

SMOKING STATS IN 2004

According to the World Health Organization:

IN 2001, 46.2 MILLION ADULTS (22.8 PERCENT) IN THE
UNITED STATES WERE CURRENT SMOKERS—25.2 PERCENT
OF MEN AND 20.7 PERCENT OF WOMEN.

ABOUT A THIRD OF THE MALE ADULT GLOBAL POPULATION SMOKES.

ABOUT 15 BILLION CIGARETTES ARE SOLD DAILY, OR 10 MILLION EVERY
MINUTE.

THE TOBACCO MARKET IS CONTROLLED BY JUST A FEW
CORPORATIONS, NAMELY AMERICAN, BRITISH AND JAPANESE
MULTINATIONAL CONGLOMERATES.

MORE THAN 4,000 TOXIC OR CARCINOGENIC CHEMICALS HAVE
BEEN FOUND IN TOBACCO SMOKE.

ONE OF EVERY THREE CIGARETTES CONSUMED WORLDWIDE
IS SMOKED IN CHINA.

NAUGHTY VICES – TEN BAD THINGS THAT ARE GOOD FUN

1. DRINKING TO THE POINT OF EMBARRASSMENT
*
2. SLEEPING PAST NOON
*
3. SHOPPING ON CREDIT
*
4. SEX WITH AN EX
*
5. GAMBLING
*
6. CREAM SAUCE
*
7. CALLING IN TO WORK SICK
*
8. STAYING UP LATE
*
9. GOSSIP
*
10. PLOTTING REVENGE

"REVENGE CAN BE EXCELLENT MEDICINE."

TRICKY BUSINESS

Clearly, there are a great many perils to be avoided in the pursuit of pleasure. The complex circuitry of the brain is like a greedy octopus just waiting to get its tentacles attached to its favorite delight. Hence, caution and awareness are essential at all times. But armed with knowledge and a strong instinct for survival, the warrior hedonist can confidently stride across life's treacherous battlefields, shield up and face to the sun, in the never-ending quest for bliss and beauty.

"We are here to laugh at the odds and live our lives so well that Death will tremble to take us."

—*Charles Bukowski*

Beautiful Things

VII

"TAKE CARE OF THE LUXURIES AND THE NECESSITIES WILL TAKE CARE OF THEMSELVES."

—Dorothy Parker

LUXURIOUS LIVING

LUXURIOUS OPULENCE WAS ONCE RESERVED EXCLUSIVELY for the elite few. Pharaohs, queens and tsars lived in spectacular style in grand palaces lavishly decorated to gaudy excess while the rest of the population was relegated to the drab and dingy sidelines and could only look on from a distance, admiring, imagining and resenting. A wildly imbalanced situation to be sure, but the staggering amount of time, effort and money that went into the creation of such splendor is an indication of how immensely gratifying it is to the human soul to be surrounded by mind-numbing opulence.

Whereas the powerful royals often went overboard in their quest for regal luxury, the instinctual human attraction to beauty and splendor was not lost on the clergy. Temples, mosques and churches were deliberately constructed to inspire awe in the eyes of potential followers. In order to establish their authority and sell their religions, they had to put on a good show, so out came the golden domes, the soaring ceilings and the stained glass. The downtrodden minions who lived in their squalid and bleak little hovels were invited to drop by the local shrine for a quick lesson in religion and a little dose of spiritual reflection, but they also got a big jolt of jaw-dropping grandeur to boot. Even the concept of heaven was sold as a glorious wonderland of eternal beauty. After all, you can't expect people to spend a lifetime playing by the rules, resisting temptation and denying themselves the good life if the ultimate reward is an eternal stay in a poorly lighted auditorium.

Happily, the great luxuries of the world have trickled down through society, albeit to varying degrees. It still takes a lot of money or a world-class sugar daddy to acquire some of the finer things in life, but the quest for luxury is not to be sniffed at. If living well means pleasing the senses, then it is essential that all the senses be tended to. Great art, spectacular architecture, luxurious materials and exquisite design all help to satisfy the soul's eternal longing for heaven on earth, and they should be sought out by whatever means are available, and as often as possible.

SEVEN LANDMARKS OF SPECTACULAR EXCESS

A humble home is a nice idea, but history has shown that supreme indulgence is the way to go when it comes to the creation of a deeply satisfying palace. Though the globe is peppered with colossal castles and magnificent monuments one can visit, there are a select few that really take the cake.

CHATEAU DE VERSAILLES – FRANCE
Once described by Voltaire as "a masterpiece of bad taste and magnificence," Versailles was the vision of Louis XIV, who decided to give his grandfather's modest hunting

lodge a little facelift and ended up achieving the impossible. He created a palace as grand and monumental as his own ego.

TAJ MAHAL – AGRA, INDIA

India's symbol of eternal love is a vision of white marble and glittering opulence. It was built by the Emperor Shah Jehan and dedicated to the memory of his beloved wife, the Empress Mumtaz Mahal, who bore him fourteen children and then promptly checked out.

NEUSCHWANSTEIN CASTLE – BAVARIA, GERMANY

Known as "The Castle of the Fairy Tale King," this little number in Bavaria was built by Mad King Ludwig, a bit of a loon who wanted to retreat from the world into a magical wonderland of his own. Hence the nifty, secret underground grotto with the floating swan boats.

THE WINTER PALACE – ST. PETERSBURG, RUSSIA

Originally built for the Empress Elizabeth between 1754 and 1762, the construction took so long that Liz was dead by the time it was completed. But Catherine the Great moved right in with her stable of boy toys, and a great time was had by all.

THE FORBIDDEN CITY – BEIJING, CHINA

The Imperial Palace of the Ming and Qing dynasties, this walled city unto itself is one of the world's largest palace complexes. For 500 years, the royal families lived in splendid isolation behind the gilded gates until the last emperor was unceremoniously driven out in 1924.

TOPKAPI PALACE – ISTANBUL, TURKEY

More than just a private residence for the sultans of the Ottoman Empire, the Topkapi Palace was also the seat of government and had ample quarters for the sultan's harem and the eunuchs who guarded them. Interestingly, all the chosen eunuchs were black so that if any of the women had an affair and a baby was born, the jig was up.

THE VATICAN – VATICAN CITY, ITALY

The world's premiere boys' club is home to the Holy Father and houses one of the world's largest collections of funny hats. Though the art, the architecture and the elaborate rituals are very beautiful and highly impressive, the parties leave much to be desired.

ESSENTIAL LUXURIES

Though the average person is unlikely to end up living a life of regal excess, there are sensible luxuries that can be acquired to indulge the senses and make life just a bit more pleasant. The following checklist of essential elements should be incorporated pronto into the life of any self-respecting hedonist:

1. HIGH THREAD-COUNT SHEETS	6. A FLASHY WARDROBE
2. GOOD WINE	7. A GOOD LOVER
3. FRESH FLOWERS	8. A PASSPORT
4. JEWELS	9. A HAMMOCK
5. REGULAR SPA TREATMENTS	10. A COCKTAIL ROBE

FIVE SOOTHING
DECORATING MOTIFS

One of the most powerful things a modern hedonist can do is to create a private space where thoughts of debt, obligation, work, drama and stress have no place. Calming music replaces the drone of the television, wind chimes tinkle in the breeze and a nice motif can set the right tone.

1. OPIUM DEN

Lots of red and black, pillows, oriental imagery and a big fat hookah pipe conjure up images of French colonial rule back in the day.

2. ZEN RETREAT

Minimalism, clean lines and a patch of sand symbolize the meaninglessness of everything. An effective affront to capitalism.

3. WHITE PALACE

Purity of theme in candles, fabrics, drapes and walls makes for complete serenity in the tradition of the modern day spa. Obvious? Yes, but minimalism and simplicity are always calming.

4. PSYCHEDELIC WONDERLAND

Day-glo furs, geometric patterns and camp art make the spirit giddy. Kitschy perhaps, but humor always wards off self-importance.

5. BOMBAY DREAM

Exotic tapestries, sequins, silks and white marble elicit images of an exotic wonderland of naughty delights.

FIVE HIGH-END TOUCHES FOR THE HOME

For those with a little cash on hand, there are a few additional elements that will help nudge the average home over the top and transform it into something a bit more spiffy.

1. CAMELS AND PEACOCKS CAN REALLY ADD DRAMA TO AN OTHERWISE UNINSPIRED GARDEN.

2. WHITE MARBLE MAKES FOR A SEXY BATHTUB AND A STURDY TOILET.

3. A ROOFTOP HELICOPTER LANDING PAD IS A HIGHLY CONVENIENT LURE FOR CELEBRITY GUESTS.

4. EXTREMELY SEXY SERVANTS ARE ALWAYS WORTH THE EXTRA MONEY.

5. IN-HOME SCREENING ROOMS ENSURE THAT YOU'LL ALWAYS GET THE BEST SEATS.

> "I don't get out of bed for less than ten thousand dollars."
> —*Linda Evangelista, supermodel*

DECADENT DELICACIES

Culinary delicacies are so defined for a variety of reasons. Sometimes it's because of the amount of effort required to procure the substance, sometimes it's an elaborate refinement process and sometimes it's simply because pretending to adore disgusting things elevates the upper classes from the Cheez Whiz–squirting bourgeoisie.

CAVIAR: Eggs are removed from a fish belly, placed on a

cracker, topped with egg whites and inserted into your belly. Now you are glamorous.

ESCARGOT: Slathered in melted butter and herbs, the slippery little snails will pass through you faster than they ever traveled on their own.

FOIE GRAS: Goose or duck pate that is not unlike glorified liverwurst. White wine helps control the retching.

FROG'S LEGS: The French just love their *cuisses de grenouilles*—prepared with butter, garlic and parsley—so much that they reportedly consume 3,500 tons of legs each year.

SEA URCHINS: The small, spiky marine animals are boiled like an egg and cracked open, and their salty little eggs and sex organs are served up like sushi. A highly undignified ending.

PRETTY YOUNG PEOPLE — THE SEASON'S BEST ACCESSORY

Madonna knew it all along, and so did Jack Nicholson. Where have you been? Demi Moore, Donald Trump, Marlene Dietrich, Warren Beatty, Cher and Pablo Picasso have had no qualms about loving the lithe and the lively, so why should you? In the current climate of youth obsession, is it any wonder that a youthful lover should become the ultimate sign of success, prestige and eternal youth? Sure there are those who raise an eyebrow at the May-December thing, but a true hedonist does not make decisions based on the assumed reactions of the dull and the dim-witted. The fact is that a hot young lover can shave years off of you physically just as easily as they can shave the gray hair off your back.

The ancient Greeks and Romans considered it a given. Drink from the fountain of youth and ye shall stay forever young. It's not about a magical or mystical trans-ference of energy, it's about a good, vigorous workout, which any trainer worth his salt will tell you is the key to staying young. Granted, the stereotype of the gold-digger and the wheelchair-bound bazillionaire is a tired cliché, but the hooking up of a sexy and powerful adult with a young and eager apprentice is a very sexy propo-sition for both parties.

In the ideal scenario, the elder partner's wisdom and experience are alluring assets that complement their physical appeal, making the whole package devasta-tingly attractive. The younger partner brings an innocent and enthusiastic sexual availability and a fresh perspec-tive to the equation, which can undercut and defuse the jaded boredom of the advancing years. In the end, every-body wins.

Inevitably the chorus will chime in. "What about equa-nimity? What about an even playing field? What about common references?" Well, granted, it can be very annoying if your lover has never even heard of Duran

Duran, but every conflict is an opportunity if we listen to the sages. Your lover may not grasp your cultural references, but do you always recognize which Mouseketeer pop star they are enthralled with? No. The trick, on both sides of the fence, is to feign interest. Your old news is new to them, and their news is . . . well, just play along.

As any Roman Caesar would tell you, young flesh is better flesh. Emotional vulnerability is sexy, and naiveté can be wildly endearing. It all hearkens back to the age-old teacher-mentor thing. The master learns from the student, and on the flip side it can be tremendously beneficial for the youthful student to kneel before the wizened elder. *Very* beneficial. But the pursuit of youth by those who are older is a relative thing. A forty-year-old in pursuit of a nubile young lover may also be the nubile young target of an eighty-year-old suitor. And so it goes.

The bottom line is that any relationship is a match of wits, a contest of power and a search for enlightenment. So share the wisdom, share the innocence, share the joy and, to avoid those nasty rumors, share the check. Unless of course they're so damn poor and cute that you have all the cards. Then you should pay.

TEN BENEFITS OF
THE SUGAR DADDY / SUGAR MAMA PARADIGM

Though there are some who may scoff at your intergenerational love match, there are many amusing and delightful benefits to be gleaned by both parties.

150

1. PEOPLE WILL TALK ABOUT YOU

*

2. WIDE-EYED STARES BY FAMILY MEMBERS

*

3. HILARIOUS BARBS ABOUT SENILITY

*

4. CLEVER RETORTS ABOUT THUMB SUCKING

*

5. A MUTUAL NEED FOR NAPPING

*

6. FASHION TIPS FOR THE ELDER

*

7. INVESTMENT ADVICE FOR THE YOUNGER

*

8. HUMOROUS PARENT-CHILD ASSUMPTIONS BY STRANGERS

*

9. SOMEONE TO PUSH THE WHEELCHAIR

*

10. SOMEONE FOR THE NURSE TO CHAT WITH WHILE YOU'RE
SOILING YOUR INCONTINENCE PANTS

LOOKING GOOD — BUY THE OUTFIT, SCREW THE PHONE BILL

A hedonist gravitates toward pleasure and enjoys that which feels good. And on the vast menu of feel-good pleasures, none quite rivals that of feeling wanted and desired. Hence, by definition, a true hedonist will always forsake the phone bill in order to look good. If you look good, you feel good. If you feel good, you draw positive attention. If you assess the positive attention, weed out the idiots and focus on the worthy prospects, you just might find your jewel in the haystack.

Is this a suggestion that true love be forsaken for purely physical attractions? No. That would be tawdry and superficial. True love is always the ultimate goal, but in the meantime, you need to dress up that sad booty and draw toward yourself someone with a little spice. It might be someone with money or who offers adventure, or a little sexual liberation might be the key selling point. It might even be intellectual stimulation that draws you in. Whatever the lure, the point is that you need to be open to experience. Seek your pleasure, you will not be soiled. Open yourself up to experience without fear of retribution. That imaginary authority figure has dissolved. You are free.

Once this fundamental and spiritual understanding has been achieved, you need to start dressing better. Fat, skinny or anywhere in between, you need to play it up in a big and unapologetic way. Sure, you may be sexier if you lose twenty pounds, but that's no reason to apologize for who you are today. Do not wait for your imagined state of perfection before you head out on your quest for satisfaction. There are countless celebrities with big butts, crooked smiles, weird profiles and beady eyes who have achieved sex symbol status. How does this happen, you ask? It's because they refuse to apologize for their shortcomings, that's why. They embrace that which makes them unique rather than shrinking from it. So dress your mess up, put it out there and never apologize.

"Clothes make the man. Naked people have little or no influence on society."
—*Mark Twain*

TEN WILDLY IMPORTANT THINGS TO PUT
ON THE CREDIT CARD

1. SPA TREATMENTS

2. AIRFARE

3. EXPENSIVE DINNERS

4. A WET BAR

5. WATCHES AND JEWELRY

6. FABULOUS FURNITURE

7. FORMAL WEAR

8. A CAR SERVICE

9. ART

10. BALANCES FROM OTHER CREDIT CARDS

CELEBRITY EXCESS

When it comes to inspired greed, outrageous demands and ridiculous requests, one need only look to the stars for inspiration. No, not the heavens. We are speaking of the spoiled divas and divos who reside in the glittering galaxy of celebrity. It would appear that there is a direct correlation between the level of one's fame and the creature comforts required to make life tolerable for these tender and sensitive flowers of the spotlight.

But really, how could Britney be expected to take to the stage and shake her moneymaker with any conviction whatsoever if her delicate constitution were to be offended by the wrong color of tulips? And imagine the devastation to the hem of Lenny Kravitz's floor-length cardigan if there was no one to follow behind carrying it like the queen's cape. And imagine the humiliation if Sean "Puffy" Combs were to be seen carrying his own umbrella. It would be unbearable, so he has someone do that for him.

Yes, the media darlings we love and hate with equal zeal are like beacons in the night, drawing us ever closer to a hedonistic utopia where one's every wish is some poor sod's command. Now let us examine just a few of the select items demanded by the elite for their backstage dressing rooms, as stipulated in their meticulously crafted contracts:

JENNIFER LOPEZ

WHITE ROOM	YELLOW ROSES WITH RED TRIM
WHITE FLOWERS	GREEN SEEDLESS GRAPES
WHITE TABLES AND/OR TABLECLOTHS	PINEAPPLE
WHITE DRAPES	PAPAYA
WHITE CANDLES	HONEYDEW MELON
WHITE COUCH	CHOCOLATE CHIP COOKIES
WHITE LILIES	VCR AND CD PLAYER
WHITE ROSES	NO TOMATO, APPLE OR GRAPE JUICES

ELTON JOHN

SIX-FOOT COUCH

LOVESEAT

2 EASY CHAIRS

2 TABLE LAMPS

4 LARGE GREEN PLANTS

1 LARGE ARRANGEMENT
OF COLORED FLOWERS
(NO CHRYSANTHEMUMS, LILIES,
CARNATIONS OR DAISIES)

HOT WATER KETTLE

ASSORTMENT OF TEAS

UNCUT LEMONS

6 CUPS, SAUCERS, PLATES
(STONEWARE)

KNIVES, FORKS AND SPOONS
(NOT PLASTIC)

12 DRINKING GLASSES
(NO PLASTIC)

MARIAH CAREY

1 BOTTLE OF CRISTAL
CHAMPAGNE—CHILLED

A SELECTION OF LOW-FAT BREADS

2 BOTTLES OF CAMUS
WHITE WINE

1 BOX OF BENDY STRAWS

LEMON ZINGER HONEY TEA

4 CHAMPAGNE GLASSES

4 WINE GLASSES

TEA SERVICE FOR EIGHT—MUST
USE POLAND SPRING WATER

2 HOT AIR HUMIDIFIERS

1 HONEY BEAR HONEY

2 AIR PURIFIERS

1 BAG OF RICOLA
THROAT LOZENGES

1 LARGE VANITY MIRROR

A SELECTION OF
SUGARLESS GUMS

12 BATH SIZE FLUFFY TOWELS

A SELECTION OF
LOW-FAT CHEESES

3 BOXES OF TISSUES

CHRISTINA AGUILERA

10 BOTTLES OF ROOM TEMPERATURE
BOTTLED WATER
(NOT EVIAN)

1 SIX-PACK OF COKE

4 PACKS OF CARNATION
INSTANT BREAKFAST
(ORIGINAL MALT FLAVOR)

1 SMALL CONTAINER OF NESQUIK,
CHOCOLATE FLAVOR

1 PACKAGE OF SOYA KAAS SOY
CHEESE, FULL FAT MOZZARELLA
OR CHEDDAR

1 BOTTLE OF ECHINACEA CAPSULES

1 SMALL PLATTER OF RASPBERRIES,
BLUEBERRIES, STRAWBERRIES,
PLUMS AND WHOLE BANANAS
(ALL MUST BE ORGANIC)

1 SMALL VEGGIE TRAY WITH
CARROTS, CHERRY TOMATOES,
RED PEPPERS, CAULIFLOWER,
CELERY AND JICAMA
(ALL MUST BE ORGANIC)

ASSORTED RAW ALMONDS, BANANA
CHIPS, DRIED CRANBERRIES

1 SMALL BOTTLE OF FLINTSTONES
VITAMINS WITH EXTRA VITAMIN C

PLATTER ASSORTMENT OF
GUMS AND MINTS

1 ROLL OF APS FILM / 200 SPEED
EXPOSURE

1 HALF PINT OF SMALL CURD
COTTAGE CHEESE
(KNUDSEN OR CLOVER ONLY)

4 VOTIVE CANDLES WITH MATCHES

CHOCOLATE CHIP OR OREO COOKIES

CHER

1 SMALL BOWL OF PLAIN M&MS

2 A&W ROOT BEER

1 SMALL BOWL OF MIXED NUTS

2 20 OZ. BOTTLES OF CHERRY
RUSH GATORADE

1 BOTTLE OF FINE RED WINE
(NO KENDALL JACKSON)

12 16 OZ. BLACK SOLO CUPS

1 BOTTLE OF FINE WHITE WINE
(NO KENDALL JACKSON)

1 HANDFUL OF FLEXISTRAWS

4 COKES

2 CUBE-SHAPED BOXES OF WHITE
ALOE KLEENEX TISSUES

4 DIET COKES

1 LARGE ASSORTMENT OF FRESH-
CUT LILIES OR GARDENIAS

6 DR. PEPPERS

1 WIG ROOM

It should be noted that the very act of making a list of demands is counter-intuitive to a relaxed life of leisure, but if you're going to be touring the world with an entourage of hundreds and Pepsi's bankrolling the whole thing, well, what the hell?

Unnecessary Dreams

VIII

"WE ARE LIKE PEOPLE LOOKING FOR SOMETHING
THEY HAVE IN THEIR HANDS ALL THE TIME;
WE'RE LOOKING IN ALL DIRECTIONS EXCEPT AT
THE THING WE WANT, WHICH IS PROBABLY WHY
WE HAVEN'T FOUND IT."

—Plato

WINNING IS FOR LOSERS —
JUST PLAY

IF, DEAR READER, YOU WILL ALLOW YOUR AUTHOR TO abandon his dialectic and switch briefly into the first person, a small story awaits that largely inspired the book you now hold before you. It is a shining example of how inspiration and revelation can spring from the most unlikely places when one is blissfully floating along with no ambition whatsoever.

On a recent visit to Barcelona with a friend, I was amused to find that many businesses really do close shop for several hours in the middle of the day. The happy and friendly residents of the city tend not to go out to dinner until nine or ten in the evening, and it's customary to head out for a drink some time around midnight. My friend and I were told by the hotel staff that no one goes to dance clubs before two in the morning. Armed with typical American skepticism, we assumed that this meant that the clubs don't really get hopping until about two in the morning. Cut to: Two American tourists standing alone in a cavernous dance club at 1:45.

To the swarthy and sexy residents of this seaside city, it seemed only logical that the hours between midnight and two were for socializing at bars. Then when the bars close at two, if the urge to dance is stronger than the urge to retire, off you go. And so it went, usually until about six in the morning.

After several nights of such debauchery, my friend and I found ourselves in conversation with the manager of our hotel. Naively, we asked him, "How does anybody get any work done if they close the businesses in the middle of the day and go out partying every night until the early morning?" The look of pity on his face spoke volumes. He smiled and confided in a most delightfully resigned manner, "You know, in America you are all in this mad race to be number one. And you know what? You win! You can be number one. Here, we would rather enjoy our lives."

The statement was simple, but the truth it touched upon was a significant one. The frantic race to be number one is a sad and desperate compulsion. Whatever happened to just playing the game? Don't parents teach that to their children? When did the rules change? When did it become a disappointment for an Olympic athlete to win a silver medal? Is happiness reserved exclusively for the one individual who places first, and everyone else is expected to shrink back in shame and disappointment? Who's the genius who came up with that perspective?

CAN GLORY BE FOUND BEYOND THE WINNER'S CIRCLE?

Of course, it can! To truly understand the larger principle behind this tantalizing question, we need look no further than to the story of one Anna Kournikova. The lovely little Lolita of the tennis world has never won a major singles tournament. Yeah, yeah, she and Martina Hingis won some doubles titles, but let us not veer off the subject. The point is that she never won, but she played the game to the hilt. Tennis is just a sport, after all, but so is life, so Anna sold the sports bras, posed for the calendars, did the music videos and enjoyed more than a few vigorous romances along the way. She was never number one according to the books, but that didn't stop her from becoming the highest earning female athlete in the world during her peak years. She may never have won Wimbledon, but she had a very lucrative and lovely time of it, both on and off the courts.

Actually, there are plenty of examples of "losers" going on to win big. Countless high school reunions have proven that the popular kids, who seemed at the time to have it all, often go on to lead crushingly dull lives while the geeky nerd in the back row goes on to build a fortune and the tall, goofy chick with the big lips becomes a supermodel. The lesson to be drawn from all this is that peaking too early in the game can be an ominous victory at best. It is far better to wait and see how the cards play out in the long run. So here's to coming in second, losing the big one, having to wait and all the other fantastic disappointments that can lead to spectacular success.

CLAY AIKEN: He lost the *American Idol* title to the velvet teddy bear but went on to find a saucy new haircut and a surprisingly large audience for his particular brand of music. Go figure.

VANESSA WILLIAMS: She won the Miss America crown, but then had it snatched from atop her carefully coiffed head when a few lezzie photos taken back in the day surfaced. Unfazed and clearly empowered by the "scandal," she went on to become a major star, easily eclipsing all the other title-holders who dutifully maintained the extremely dull moral standards of the crown.

SUSAN LUCCI: She rose to legendary status in the world of soap operas after losing the Best Actress Emmy for thirteen consecutive years. When she finally won the damn thing, she fell off the celebrity radar completely.

MICHELLE KWAN: The beloved ice minx has won countless national and world titles but has twice been denied the much-coveted Olympic gold medal, once by a boozy Russian and a second time by a tiny terror from Texas. Her stoic strength in the face of such adversity has endeared her to millions, but she may still go for the gold a third time. If she really does win, it could be Lucciville for Ms. Kwan.

HARRISON FORD: After a promising debut in a small role in *American Graffiti*, Ford was unable to find another promising gig for nearly ten years, during which he patiently worked as a carpenter, far-removed from Hollywood's inner circle. After his decade-long hiatus, he nabbed a role in a little film called *Star Wars* and went on to become box-office gold.

ALBERT EINSTEIN: Talk about a slow starter. One of the

"Be content with your lot;
one cannot be first in everything."
—*Aesop*

greatest geniuses of all time, Einstein couldn't speak properly until he was four years old, and he couldn't read until he was seven. Evaluated as being well behind all the children around him, young Albert gave his parents pause, but he eventually came up with some pretty nifty ideas.

BILL GATES, DAVID GEFFEN AND TED TURNER: This trio of staggeringly successful businessmen all share a common bond. No, they didn't graduate at the top of their classes, nor were they chosen as valedictorians. They all dropped out, flunked out or were kicked out of college.

HEROES AND ROLE MODELS

Somewhere along the line, as literature and deductive reasoning have given way to hysterical moral debates and reduced attention spans, heroes seem to have fallen out of favor and the dreaded "role model" has stepped into the spotlight. This dubious title is not so much earned as it is thrust upon athletes, celebrities and public figures. But if priests, politicians and scoutmasters can't always live up to the title, why would anyone look to jocks and rock stars as exemplary models of behavior?

As if this ridiculous title was not burdensome enough for humans, it is now being ascribed to fictional characters as well. As recently as May 2004, a Senate Commerce Committee hearing was held to harass the Motion Picture Association of America into decreasing smoking in the movies and slapping an R rating on any film that depicted characters smoking. As usual, excessive violence, gore and general stupidity are perfectly fine, but historical accuracy and realistic character portrayals have no place in cinema or television.

The television sitcoms of yesteryear offer a tantalizing glimpse of a time when drinking and smoking weren't shrouded in shame and judgment. On *Bewitched,* Darrin was frequently greeted by Samantha after a hard day at the ad agency with a good stiff drink. On *The Mary Tyler Moore Show*, Mr. Grant kept a bottle of whiskey in his desk drawer, and even the Howells managed to produce umbrella-topped cocktails on *Gilligan's Island.* Lucy and Desi smoked, as did Rob and Laura on *The Dick Van Dyke Show*, and even Andy Griffith lit up on occasion. Granted, this was before the hazards of smoking became general knowledge, but the point is that the characters accurately depicted the behaviors of their day. Will reruns soon show the cocktails and cigarettes blurred out with pixelation like Janet Jackson's society-scarring right bosom?

Since those carefree days, it has been decided that the population at large was entirely mindless and tended to ape whatever behaviors they saw on the screen. Hence, characters on television needed to be role models and a sweeping sanitization swept across network television. Though things have loosened up a bit in recent years, it

"When you are content to be simply yourself and don't compare or compete, everybody will respect you."
—*Lao Tzu*

is usually only the secondary characters, if any, who are depicted as indulging in any sort of excess, while the central characters look on in mild disapproval.

In the 1990s, the British sitcom *Absolutely Fabulous* became a huge international hit with its central characters Patsy and Edina exhibiting virtually every vice known to womankind. That was what made it funny—two middle-aged women desperately clinging to their youth through excessive indulgence, unbridled hedonism and general debauchery. In the United States, several networks attempted to create an American version of the show, but British humor rarely crosses the Atlantic unscathed, and none ever saw the light of day. Why? Because network television is dependent upon corporate sponsorship, and most of the behaviors the characters so gleefully engaged in would have resulted in advertising withdrawals and boycotts by the moral militias.

AbFab did air on Comedy Central, and shockingly there was no surge in drunken driving, coke-sniffing or depraved excess among middle-aged women in the U.S. and the U.K. There was simply a lot of laughter as audiences delighted in the ridiculous adventures of two *fictional* characters. Somehow the audience was able to deduce that it wasn't real and that there is humor to be found in the full spectrum of human foibles.

As a general rule, it is risky business to model oneself

after another person. Not only are you underestimating your own abilities to judge and decide, but you are gambling with your own individuality, which may ultimately be your greatest asset. As for modeling oneself after fictional characters, that is the true sign of a moron.

CHASING FAME — ANONYMITY IS THE ULTIMATE LUXURY

A particular and peculiar sickness of the Western world has emerged over the course of the last century and gotten a stranglehold on the sensibilities of the populace at large. It is rooted in a deeply misguided notion that fame and celebrity are the ultimate ideals. People allow themselves to be televised eating maggots, searching for true love from a sad selection of spotlight-starved contestants or even showering on a webcam in order to achieve some sort of vague and elusive validation. To be on television is to matter, and to live a life undocumented is to live a life invisible. But fame is not what it used to be.

In the early half of the twentieth century, being famous was both glamorous and rare. And though Marilyn Monroe, Montgomery Clift and that saucy, suicidal spitfire Lupe Velez might argue otherwise, it was a relative cakewalk compared to what fame entails in the present day. Gone are the days of the grand illusion and personal privacy. And as Andy Warhol predicted, "In the future, everyone will be famous for fifteen minutes." He was right. As these words are being typed, publicists from Los Angeles to New York are downing countless martinis trying desperately to maintain the "celebrity status" of failed game show contestants, tabloid sex pigs and famed murderers. And nowadays, celebrity does not necessarily mean riches. If extreme wealth actually does enter into the picture, things only get worse. Famous actors and athletes are relentlessly pursued by paparazzi in hopes that they will throw up in public or be caught in a surprising and shocking sexual tryst. Elevation equals character assassination, and the famous find themselves stalked to the point of peril. Still, the masses crave the spotlight.

So now careers in politics, sports or entertainment have serious consequences, and the fortunes to be made are often squandered on security details. The true luxury of the twenty-first century is anonymity. Though being recognized on the street may help to quell lingering resentments of high school snubs and oversights, the loss of privacy and freedom has changed the equation immeasurably. There is tremendous power in being able to enter a bar anywhere in the world and be a stranger. To be able to misbehave badly in public and have no one remember is a gift. And to have the freedom to go to the supermarket wildly hung over and not be photographed, well, you don't know what you've got 'til it's gone.

So, the next time you find yourself dreaming of stardom, stop and give it a second thought. You may be far better off than you think.

THE PROS OF BEING FAMOUS

GETTING A TABLE WITHOUT A RESERVATION

GETTING MORE ATTENTION THAN YOUR FRIENDS

GETTING LAID WITHOUT HAVING TO TRY

PAID APPEARANCES

TOP-OF-THE-LINE AIRBRUSHING

PHOTOGRAPHIC APPROVAL

HAVING "PEOPLE" TO SAY NO FOR YOU

HUGE PAYCHECKS

DELUSIONS OF SELF-IMPORTANCE

THE PERSONAL STYLIST

"WORSHIP ME!"

THE CONS OF BEING FAMOUS

STRANGERS THINKING THEY KNOW YOU

STALKERS

LAWYER FEES

COUSINS SEEKING CASH

LOSS OF PRIVACY

EXCESSIVE SCRUTINY REGARDING YOUR APPEARANCE

UNFLATTERING PHOTOGRAPHS

KISS-AND-TELL LOVERS

SPECULATION AND GOSSIP

EXTRA SCRUTINY WHEN RENTING PORNOGRAPHY

"I'M ONLY HUMAN."

STRIVING FOR PERFECTION

"Have no fear of perfection,
you'll never reach it."
—Salvador Dali

At this point we come upon yet another truly annoying archetype in the gallery of clichés—the perfectionist— seated on the grand dais directly beside the martyr and the Pollyanna, and no doubt stewing about not being placed center stage. The perfectionist is hopelessly addicted to control and is by nature incapable of recognizing that which truly matters and that which is truly irrelevant. *Everything must be perfect!!!*

This quest for perfection, whether in terms of personal appearance, work performance or everyday details, can have serious consequences: say for example, a prolonged stay at a minimum-security women's prison in Connecticut where the sheets and the floral arrangements are far below acceptable standards. What goes around comes around, and by demanding flawless perfection from others, you may be inviting those around you to zero in on that one chink in your own armor that will ultimately bring you down.

Of course, not every perfectionist imposes his or her unrealistic standards on others. Some are perfectly happy to apply the unrealistic demands only unto themselves. What these sad souls fail to recognize is that perfection is highly unattractive. It is the flaws and imperfections in people that make them endearing. It is the cartoon character with the oversized head and utter lack of self-awareness that we love and root for. It is the singer whose voice cracks with emotion who moves us, not the plastic crooner who hits every note with a smug and self-satisfying smile. Even in the physical realm, the greatest beauties are those who have imperfections that allow us to see the human being beneath the beautiful facade. Venus de Milo was nothing until her arms fell off.

> "Fame is proof that people are gullible."
> —*Ralph Waldo Emerson*

SUCCESS — WHAT'S THE TRUE MEASURE?

As we have seen, in the scheme of things, your moment-to-moment quality of life is equally if not more important than your long-term successes and failures. Goals are important and achievement can be extremely gratifying as well as lucrative, but if in the course of your endeavors you have been an overworked, humorless and relentlessly driven maniac, then you have not been successful.

A successful life cannot be measured in numbers. A hefty bank account is a very nice thing, and a wall full of awards may impress the dinner guests, but those are signs of a successful career, and not necessarily a successful life. Your career is not your life. It may be a large part of it, and that's fine as long as you have enjoyed the ride and balanced it alongside your personal relationships and sufficient leisure time with a healthy dose of perspective. But if your desire to succeed has become all-consuming, eclipsed all else and prevented you from truly enjoying every day, then you have missed the proverbial boat.

If you want to measure just how successful you have been in constructing your life, then answer the following questions honestly and you will get a very clear picture:

DO YOU HAVE STABLE, DRAMA-FREE PERSONAL RELATIONSHIPS?

DO YOU LAUGH OUT LOUD EVERY DAY?

DO YOU INSTINCTIVELY CLEAR TIME IN YOUR DAY FOR LEISURE?

DO YOU SLEEP WELL AT NIGHT?

DO YOU REWARD YOURSELF FOR YOUR OWN SUCCESSES?

DO YOU MAKE THE MOST OF YOUR SURROUNDINGS?

ARE YOU ABLE TO TRUST PEOPLE?

DO YOU ENJOY DOING NOTHING?

ARE YOU ABLE TO LOVE FREELY?

ARE YOU ABLE TO BE AFFECTIONATE?

DO YOU LIVE WITHOUT FEAR?

Not all of the traits listed above come easily or naturally to everyone, and some may require a conscious effort. But as lifestyles go, they are all worth aspiring to if you truly want to enjoy your time on earth and be successful in living your life.

ZERO FAT = ZERO FUN

One of the greatest pleasure-squashers in today's society is the current obsession with health, longevity, dieting and body-fat reduction. It is perfectly natural and really quite practical to want to look and feel good and to remain fit. But to live under the delusion that zero body fat will bring you happiness is laughable at best. Granted, if you suddenly gain a hundred pounds, your desirability on the open market may sink dramatically, but a few pounds here and there make no difference whatsoever. The assumption that everyone else is monitoring your physique against some imagined standard of perfection is indicative of a massively inflated ego. No one cares if you have dessert now and then. No one notices when you gain or lose three pounds. And if by chance there is someone in your life who does notice, is keeping track and commenting on such things, it's not your eating habits you should be concerned with so much as your choice of friends and/or lovers.

For some, a slow metabolism, a genetic predisposition or certain health conditions may make some restrictions necessary, and in such cases health matters always come before indulgence. But regardless of your body type, the idea that being stick-thin will make you happier and help you live longer is a false one. You can cut the fat off that pork chop and eat all the nasty, fat-free soy snacks you want, but that won't make you feel any better about yourself. You may decide that yakking up your dinner in the bathroom is the answer, but when your teeth go gray and your hair starts falling out, you may end up rethinking things.

The fact is that your body needs some fat to protect your cells, so again, don't try to outsmart Mother Nature. If you want to be slim and healthy, eat real food at regular intervals, keep the portions sensible, and get some exercise. Do not obsess, do not resort to extreme measures and don't become that annoying person at dinner who has a long list of dietary restrictions and orders everything on the side. It's unnecessary, and it hurts the chef's feelings.

LIVE WELL, LIVE LONG

LIFERS: PABLO, GEORGIE, AND MUMSIE

As each of us has an entirely unique genetic code and metabolism, it is entirely possible that what is good for your neighbor may kill you, and the things you love to indulge in might hospitalize your neighbor. But one thing seems to hold true. Those who enjoy the pleasures that life has to offer not only live better, sometimes they even live longer. Once again, irony illustrates that we must all decide what is best for our own life and that following someone else's prescription may be entirely futile.

PICASSO
LIVED TO BE: 91 YEARS OLD

Talk about following your bliss, Picasso spent a lifetime dedicated to his art and to expressing his inner self, both dark and light. A compulsive smoker, drinker and an incorrigible womanizer, Picasso lived by his own rules, thumbed his nose at convention and never gave up any of his favorite vices.

GEORGE BURNS
LIVED TO BE: 100 YEARS OLD

Known for his trademark cigars and deadpan humor, Burns often joked about performing on his one hundredth birthday. His life's work was laughter, and it kept him going for a full century, and through it all he never denied himself his favorite pastimes of drinking, smoking cigars and ogling young women.

THE QUEEN MOTHER
LIVED TO BE: 102 YEARS OLD

England's beloved Queen Mum actually led a complicated life, living through wars, political turmoil and the premature death of her husband. But a wry sense of humor, a love of horse racing, a tendency toward bank overdrafts and a passion for tippling kept the lady dowager in good spirits throughout. Known for her love of gin and tonics in the morning, the tiny lady in the silly hat was a true master of the sustained buzz. To celebrate her hundredth birthday, a cake was served with her favorite icing made of gin and sugar.

Living well may not guarantee a long life, but neither does living a life of self-restraint. In the cases of Picasso, George Burns and the Queen Mum, it would appear that each was keenly in touch with his or her internal barometer of pleasure. Life may have presented them all with times of great stress, but their natural instinct was to create their own moments of pleasure and satisfaction, which in turn ensured that the turbulent times were balanced by equal times of still and calm.

Still and Calm

IX

"OUTSIDE NOISY, INSIDE EMPTY."
— *Chinese Proverb*

NIGHT SKIES AND
SECLUDED BEACHES

MAKE NO MISTAKE ABOUT IT, HEDONISTS LOVE THE nightlife. Flashing lights, seductively pulsating rhythms and time spent in highly stylized nightspots with the "in crowd" have an undeniable appeal. Even so, there is another side to the coin. Balance is and has always been the key to a supremely satisfying existence.

Any resident of a major urban metropolis will tell you that the key to sanity is escaping the hustle and bustle every now and again. Country retreats, beach homes and tropical vacations offer more than just a change of scenery, they offer a change of pace. The physically calming effects of starry skies, secluded beaches, wraparound country porches and wide open spaces are not to be underestimated. And when coupled with a pitcher of mojitos, these settings become positively therapeutic. Of course these things may not be regularly affordable to most, but even the occasional weekend getaway can do wonders.

For those who, for whatever reason, simply cannot get away, there are plenty of little sanctuaries to be found within the confines of any major city. A little creativity and effort is all that is required to transform the mundane into a pleasurable affair. If you're going to have a bottle of wine with someone, have it up on the roof under the stars. If you're meeting up with an old friend, buy some crackers and cheese and go to the park rather than to a noisy and crowded restaurant. Or if you have a free afternoon, go to the museum and float back through time rather than parking it on the couch and watching television.

A good hedonist will always choose his surroundings as carefully as he chooses the right bottle of wine, and he will make a point of placing himself in the best surroundings whenever possible. Of course, being in a lovely setting with a group of idiots defeats the whole purpose, but a seasoned pleasure-seeker is a master of the upgrade and is always on the lookout for a superior option. Here are just a few guidelines to keep in mind:

THE PERSON WITH THE BEST CAR ALWAYS DRIVES.

ALWAYS STAY WITH THE RELATIVE OR FRIEND WHO HAS THE POOL.

MAKE FRIENDS WITH PEOPLE WHO OWN BOATS.

MAKE FRIENDS WITH PEOPLE YOUR OWN SIZE AND MULTIPLY YOUR WARDROBE.

ALWAYS OPT FOR A TAXI OVER THE SUBWAY, ESPECIALLY WHEN DRUNK.

ALWAYS CHOOSE A BOOTH OVER A TABLE AT A RESTAURANT.

REMEMBER THAT BOUTIQUE HOTELS ARE LESS LIKELY TO HAVE SCREAMING CHILDREN.

SLEEP WITH FLIGHT ATTENDANTS TO SECURE FREE FLIGHTS.

WHEN FLYING COACH, REQUEST THE EXIT ROW FOR EXTRA LEG ROOM.

DO NOT FLY COACH.

DAILY AFFIRMATIONS

"SEXY BEAST"

Corny though they may be, daily affirmations help to reinforce belief systems and are an effective tool in the training of the mind. In order to ensure that you are making steady progress on the road to healthy hedonism, it won't hurt to remind yourself of a few truisms now and then, especially when things are getting shaky and you're feeling an uncontrollable urge to go to the gym or to work harder.

I AM A SENSUAL AND SEXY BEAST.

MY LIFE IS FAR BIGGER THAN MY JOB.

BIG OR SMALL, MY BANK ACCOUNT DOES NOT DEFINE ME.

I HAVE NO INTEREST IN SUFFERING OR SELF-DENIAL.

MY ENERGY IS VALUABLE AND IS NOT TO BE WASTED.

I AM MY OWN SANTA CLAUS.

LIFE IS SHORT, SO I MUST DRESS WELL.

IF I WANT IT THEN IT MUST BE RIGHT.

REALITY IS HIGHLY OVERRATED.

SOBRIETY IS ALWAYS AN OPTION.

TEN BEST PLACES TO THINK

The antithesis of staggering along on life's treadmill is the state of absolute quiet and reflection. Continuous obsession about business, world news and the lives of others prevents us from taking the time to look at the big picture of our own lives. Whether achieved through solitary silence or through thoughtful conversations with those closest to us, introspection, honest evaluation and positive visualization are essential to achieving a state of true happiness. You can run all you like, you can move to the other side of the world and you can ditch those who encourage you to look within, but you can never escape yourself.

Everyone needs some quiet time when the chaos of the surrounding world falls away, when thoughts of debt, disappointment and judgment dissolve, and when you ask yourself what you truly want in life. Chances are that dreams of material acquisitions will lose some of their luster, and more attainable things such as friendship, creative opportunity, love, adventure, inner peace and freedom from stress will come out on top. How you can realize these forms of fulfillment remains to be determined, but the puzzle will be more easily solved in tranquil and pleasant surroundings. So, what are the best settings for the grand introspection?

1. AT THE EDGE OF THE OCEAN

2. DURING BUSINESS MEETINGS

3. ON THE ROOF

4. IN THE BATHTUB

5. ON THE PORCH

6. LYING IN THE GRASS

7. ON A TRAIN

8. OVER MORNING COFFEE

9. AT THE BAR

10. IN A DUTCH COFFEE SHOP

TEN ATMOSPHERIC ESSENTIALS

When it comes to enjoying your favorite pleasures, the right ambiance can enhance the experience immeasurably, and there are certain atmospheric essentials that no hedonist worth her salt should be without. Just a few household basics will go a long way toward transforming any home into a smoothly running pleasure palace. Remember, it's all about comfort, beauty and continuous intoxication of the senses, no matter how subtle.

1. A FIREPLACE IN WINTER	6. MULTIPLE PILLOWS
2. CANDLES WHEN IT RAINS	7. CLEAN WINDOWS
3. AIR CONDITIONING IN SUMMER	8. A WARM AND COZY BED
4. SOFT LIGHTING	9. PLANTS AND FLOWERS
5. GOOD MUSIC	10. ART

SIESTA — THE LOST ART OF SLEEPING

When a corporate CEO reveals in an interview that he gets eight hours of sleep every night, as Jeff Bezos of Amazon.com did in the *Wall Street Journal*, and it becomes big news, something is seriously askew in the collective unconscious. If sufficient sleep has become a status symbol, then Armageddon must be closer than we think. If basic biological functions are now considered luxuries, it's only a matter of time before pooping registers as the height of prestige activities.

Regardless of external obligations and tightly packed calendars, it is a primary duty of any hedonist to get sufficient sleep. There is nothing in the universe that maintains youth, reduces stress and retains sanity with so little effort required. You just lie down, lose consciousness and rake in the rewards. What could be easier? It certainly beats twenty minutes on the treadmill. When life offers up a supremely pleasurable leisure activity that also has inherent health benefits, it should be embraced with open arms and a sequined sleeping mask.

Napping, snoozing, siesta, slumber—all beautiful words for a beautiful pastime. But in order to turn sleeping into a true art form, proper respect must be given to the sandman, for he is among your very best of friends.

TREAT YOUR BED WITH THE RESPECT IT DESERVES AS A SHRINE TO UNCONSCIOUSNESS.

RESPECT MOTHER NATURE BY SLEEPING IN THE ALTOGETHER.

BE NOT SELFISH—SHARE THY BED FREELY.

EXCEPT WHEN NECESSARY, REMOVE THE ALARM CLOCK FROM SIGHT, FOR IT IS EVIL.

INVEST IN A PROPER NIGHT TABLE AND KEEP IT WELL-STOCKED WITH BEDSIDE ACCOUTERMENT.

KEEP A SLEEPING MASK BENEATH THE PILLOW FOR UNREASONABLY SUNNY MORNINGS.

**ALWAYS KEEP EARPLUGS CLOSE BY IN CASE YOUR LATEST
"FRIEND" SNORES LIKE A WILDEBEEST.**

**GIVE YOUR BED A NAME, CONFIDE IN IT AND
SHOWER IT WITH PRAISE.**

"There is a time for many words, and there is also a time for sleep."
—*Homer*

**CHOOSE QUALITY BEDDING AND KEEP A VARIETY OF BLANKETS
TO SUIT YOUR MOOD.**

**CHOOSE QUALITY LOVERS AND KEEP A VARIETY ON HAND TO
SUIT YOUR MOOD.**

SOBER PLEASURES

Lest the mistaken impression be given that life's good times always require a chemical jump start, it should be noted that a good buzz can be just as easily attained in complete sobriety. The menu of life's pleasures is long and varied, and it could easily be argued that many of them are best experienced with complete clarity of mind.

As the ancient sages have pointed out countless times, the pursuit of the higher pleasures, or the state of nirvana, is ultimately a spiritual quest. This is not to be confused with a religious quest, for religion is another matter entirely. Spirituality is a personal matter, not a political one. And each of us is entitled to define it in our own terms. If your spirituality is the connection you feel to the awesome power of nature when climbing a mountain, great. If it's the giddy high you get from shoe shopping, so be it. Whatever it is, it all comes down to a simple truth. You don't need chemicals to get high. So here is a mere sampling of the many ways you can achieve a great buzz without booze:

TRAVELING   ARTISTIC EXPRESSION

SEX   EXTREME SPORTS

COMMUNING WITH NATURE   YOGA OR MEDITATION

SHOPPING   SPA TREATMENTS

FINE DINING   CONVERSATION AND LAUGHTER

WATER - FLOATING FREELY

The genuinely calming and soothing effects of being submerged in liquid can be directly traced back to the embryonic state. In the womb, we float freely, in silence, sensing only the distant vibrations of the outside world. As our brains form, we come to know this state of true peace and it becomes our earliest experience of Shangri-la. Then we are unceremoniously squeezed through a narrow portal, exposed to the cold, harsh air, we throw up and get smacked on the ass. Thus begins the trauma of life.

Therefore it is no wonder that we all have a deeply rooted desire to return to the womb—in the figurative sense, of course. This instinctive human impulse is not lost on real estate developers who build hotels by the sea, home owners with extra cash who quickly install swimming pools, and day spas that create swirling Jacuzzis to pamper their clients. Both as a species and as individuals, we emerged from the water, and it is by returning to the water that we find an inexplicable comfort.

A good hedonist never stays on dry land too long. For a quick fix, a bob in the water provides instant relaxation. Second only to sleep, it the easiest and quickest way to relieve stress and drift into a state of peaceful surrender. So take a bath, sink into the hot tub, lie in a stream, jump in the pool or just have a nice, long float in the ocean whenever possible. With each immersion into the silent embrace of the water, you will be one step closer to your personal nirvana.

Nirvana - Take it or Leave it

X

"WHETHER OR NOT WE USE IT, IT GOES."

— Phillip Larkin
on life

SO WHAT EXACTLY IS THIS NIRVANA BUSINESS?

NIRVANA IS A TERM THAT IS OFTEN CASUALLY TOSSED ABOUT, and as a result its true definition has become somewhat murky over time. It is not a location, it is not a band—it is a state of mind. Nirvana is the Buddhist term for the quiet state of peace and pure pleasure that can only be found in one's own private, innermost theater of experience. It is a place of escape, where life's sorrows and tribulations fall away and a state of pure bliss is experienced.

It is glimpsed in fleeting moments by the athlete who executes a flawless play of superhuman proportions, by the dancer whose movements become one with the music, and by the lone monk who achieves absolute stillness of mind and spirit. It is the ideal psychological state of harmony and peace. And it is a real bitch to attain.

Every human on the planet has an innate knowledge of nirvana, perhaps from those carefree days in the womb. The trick is to recapture that delirious feeling of safety and sheer bliss. As we have seen throughout history, attempts to return to the blessed state have involved a dizzying array of practices, but many of history's grand schemes and experiments have been far too ambitious. Permanent nirvana may be beyond our grasp, but it's nice to know that little glimmers and spectacular moments are achievable. Whether you take them or leave them is entirely up to you.

YOU CAN'T TAKE IT WITH YOU

You Can't Take It With You was a wildly successful play by George S. Kaufman and Moss Hart that went on to win a Pulitzer Prize for drama in 1936. In 1938, it was released as a film directed by Frank Capra and starring Jean Arthur, Lionel Barrymore and James Stewart. The premise was simple: A sane girl from a nutty family becomes engaged to a rich boy from a stuffy family. Misunderstandings abound as the rigid stiffs clash with free-spirited loons, discipline vies with conformity, and hilarity ensues. But the underlying message of the work itself is not so much metaphorical as it is a simple fact. Life is there for the living, and the pressure to measure up to an imagined ideal is a big bag of gas. In the end, you can't take it with you.

When applied to the lifestyle of an individual, this hokey old title takes on a profound significance. It forces the question: What are you living for? What is the point of accumulating massive wealth if you can't enjoy it? What are you building that is so important? And wouldn't you be better off leaving your children with a deeply rooted understanding that life is a spectacular adventure to be embraced, rather than leading them to believe that a swollen bank account is the key to happiness?

It may seem that serious money makes life easier, but the truth is that serious money means serious headaches. In and of itself, money without happiness is meaningless. A penniless man with true friends is wealthy, and a rich man who is isolated is truly poverty-stricken. The point is that it all evens out in the end, and if you are wise enough to recognize that all along, you can have a beautiful life regardless of your financial status. You may be broke for thirty years, but that doesn't mean you're poor. If you follow your bliss, if you value your relationships more than your bank account and if you live for the moment, you will tap into that which is the true measure of success—a truly happy life.

At this point, it must be acknowledged that your author is dancing upon the precipice of sheer corniness, but the truth is that all of the answers to life's great mysteries are painfully simple. Joy begets joy, and misery draws more of the same. Like magnets, we draw unto ourselves that which we emit and we repel that which is contrary to our mindset. Focus on the negative and you will draw more of the same into your orbit, visualize the life you want and you will slowly begin to move toward it. It's an ugly realization for the twenty-first century cynic, but it is inescapably true.

So, if you can't take it with you, it only makes sense to enjoy it while you've got it. Do not waste your power, your energy, your youth, your vitality or the moment at hand. It will all disappear before you even know it.

TEN THINGS THAT ARE TEMPORARY

1. YOUTH	**6. PROFESSIONAL IMPORTANCE**
*	*
2. ROMANTIC INFATUATION	**7. RELATIONSHIPS**
*	*
3. SIX-PACK ABS	**8. DEBT**
*	*
4. YOUR JOB	**9. HEMORRHOIDS**
*	*
5. YOUR TROUBLES	**10. LIFE ITSELF**

FEAR OF AGING

One of the most curious yet widespread neuroses of the day is a fear of growing older. Children often look forward to aging as it signifies getting the hell out sixth grade, and the same holds true as one emerges from high school and then college. However, a strange turnabout seems to take place with many twenty-nine-year-olds. Suddenly, the realization that thirty is looming causes great distress as they fully grasp the fact that contrary to what they had always believed, they are not going to be eternally young. Suddenly, they question their place in the grand picture and feel a vague and nagging pressure to be further up the ladder of success than they actually are.

How funny these little twinks are, for they do not realize that they are finally coming into their own, transforming from the oldest possible child on the planet to the youngest of adults. And their self-induced crises of achievement assessment are little more than karmic pay-back for the arrogance of youth, of which we are all guilty. And as the clock ticks on, each new milestone brings new questions and strange revelations, but the refrain is always the same. "I don't feel forty." "I don't feel sixty." "I don't feel eighty." And why would you? How exactly does one *feel* a number? The answer is that you don't, because you are the same person all along.

From the moment we pass through Mommy's little port-hole, we are all moving closer to death on a daily basis. That's not cynicism or a morbid outlook, that's just the deal. And the sooner in life we accept that simple fact, the sooner we can begin to live for the day and ensure that our lives are happy and rich with experience and laugh-ter. You know the movie's going to end at some point, but it does no good to keep checking your watch.

The two types of people who squawk the loudest about growing older are those who are clinging to the past and those who believe that youth was the only advantage they ever had in life. For the former, sentimentality has eclipsed the present, and for the latter, low self-esteem has done the same. In both cases, some serious pleasures are in order to help these sad sacks shake the blues. And the beauty of life is that it's never too late to change, so snap out of it and stop feeling sorry for yourself, because there are big things in store.

THE MUUMUU YEARS — AGING DISGRACEFULLY

We now come to the most crucial juncture of life's grand schema—old age. Conventional wisdom would have us believe that old age is a time for resolution, resignation and retirement. While this is a comfortable notion that has stood the test of time, in truth, it is entirely optional. To a true hedonist, old age is an opening of the gate, an opportunity for freedom and a free pass in the grand cosmic paradigm.

Youth is a time of torment. Are you cute enough, clever enough, ambitious enough? Decades pass quickly as the young struggle to maintain their allure and the middle-aged scramble for status. But by the time you hit seventy, who gives a shit? You have lived, you have learned, you have won and you have failed. You have wisdom and you are entitled to cut loose. But in order to fully enjoy your golden years, you must plan ahead. To age in the most fabulously disgraceful manner possible, deals must be struck in advance.

While you are young, you must identify those friends with whom you would be comfortable for a lifetime. Regardless of the marriages, careers and commitments that may arise, you must make a pact with a select few with whom you will work toward purchasing country homes around the world. Regardless of whether they are CEOs or lifelong waiters, everyone must contribute to the pot. Some will provide real estate, some will supply sexy young distractions, but everyone must bring something to the game. These are your partners in the muumuu years.

Up until the age of seventy, it is advisable to keep it together, retain your youth and build your personal empire, but once seventy hits, all bets are off. Carbohydrates, alcohol and pain killers are the name of the game, and everyone shares in the riches. At that point, everyone retires and the long, debauched slide into senility begins. Spouses, tricks and crazy strangers are welcome. A traveling loop is formed between so-and-so's place in Miami, what's-her-name's place in Monte Carlo, and thingamajig's place in the Catskills.

Whatever locations are available, the idea is that the party keeps moving, the players all participate and no flight attendant is safe from the occasional grope. The essential uniform for all, male or female, is a roomy muumuu and orthopedic flip-flops. Large, ping pong ball–size rings are encouraged if only for show. Skinny gray braids and obvious wigs are optional. Once the pretense of propriety is eliminated, and 401(k)s have been cashed out, old age can be supremely liberating, surprisingly sexy and altogether satisfying. The trick is to plan ahead. Who do you want to spend your golden years with? Make that call and make that plan.

Once a solid plan for the muumuu years is in place, life becomes infinitely easier. Knowing that a grand old time is on the horizon serves the same purpose as believing in heaven. Having something to look forward to rather than dreading a slow decline into isolation makes all the difference. It's all about having goals, after all.

ESSENTIALS FOR THE MUUMUU YEARS

A COLORFUL SELECTION OF ROOMY CAFTANS

OVERSIZED JEWELRY

SECURED REAL ESTATE

MOOD ELEVATORS

SENSIBLE SHOES

AMPLE SUPPLIES OF WINE

FLOPPY SUN HATS

ANTACIDS

A CAMERA

GOOD FRIENDS

DEATHBED REVIEW

As the morphine drips slowly through the tubes and the blurry, smiling faces of family, friends and muumuu-clad compatriots smile lovingly upon you, there will come a moment in which it all becomes vividly, unquestionably and inescapably clear. You were in the driver's seat all along. The choices that you made determined your path, the opportunities were always there and the ultimate direction of your life was in your own hands the entire time.

When the grand game finally comes to an end, there is nothing more disappointing than the crushing realization that you never reached for the golden ring. Missed opportunities, self-delusion and misplaced priorities come crashing down like shards of broken glass, reminding you of what might have been. To look back over the course of your life and to know that your days were wasted chasing after illusions and trying to impress some imaginary figure of authority who was never really there to begin with is to understand the gravity of regret.

But a sad ending is not inevitable. Regret need not accompany you to the other side. If you still have enough strength to lift the amusing and sensibly-priced book you now hold before you, then you still have the strength to change. Life is but a series of decisions, and you can decide right now to embrace the joys of leisure and pleasure that are rightfully yours. You can decide to follow your bliss and allow pleasure to be your guiding light. Hedonism is not a dirty word, nor is it an irresponsible philosophy. It is good, it is practical and it will enrich your life immeasurably. So before the dire day of reckoning arrives, take a moment to imagine yourself onstage for the final curtain call, and imagine what your answers will be in the final deathbed review. How did you live?

DID YOU LAUGH AND PLAY IN THE SUN?

DID YOU ALLOW YOURSELF TO BE FREE?

DID YOU TAKE CHANCES?

DID YOU TRUST YOUR INSTINCTS?

DID YOU TREAT YOURSELF WELL?

DID YOU TRULY CONNECT WITH THOSE AROUND YOU?

DID YOU LEARN TO GIVE WITHOUT TAKING?

DID YOU EVER LET GO OF THE PAIN?

DID YOU FORGIVE AND MOVE ON?

DID YOU LIVE OUT YOUR DREAMS?

DID YOU ATTEMPT THE IMPOSSIBLE?

DID YOU LEARN HOW TO LOVE?

DID YOU TAKE RESPONSIBILITY FOR YOUR OWN LIFE?

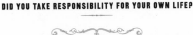

At the end of the day, it all comes down to you. No matter what your lot in life, there are moments of joy and happiness to be had. You can go out and create them, or you can sit and wallow in a state of self-perpetuated stress and misery. If you have a dream you should commit to it. If you find a vocation that you love and you want to be the very best, good luck to you. But wherever your journey leads you, remember that life is not an assignment. It is an adventure that should be filled with beauty, bliss and, above all, pleasure.

MICHAEL FLOCKER
IS THE AUTHOR OF THE
INTERNATIONAL BESTSELLER
THE METROSEXUAL GUIDE TO STYLE.
HE LIVES IN NEW YORK CITY.